THE PROVIDENCE GUIDE

91
BEST
RESTAURANTS

* **and more!**

BY DEBORAH MOXHAM AND JOHN SCHENCK

FOR HOLLY AND TED

With thanks to Nicky Nichtern for creating an inviting, user-friendly design, and to Susan A. Kaplan for her invaluable editorial contribution.

This book is also dedicated, with enormous admiration, to anyone, anyplace, who cooks for a living. There may be tougher jobs, but we can't think of one.

> **"One cannot think well,
> love well, sleep well,
> if one has not dined well."**
>
> *Virginia Woolf*

TABLE OF CONTENTS

F O R E W O R D

Few New England cities rival Providence for the quality and variety of its culinary offerings. Rich in cultural diversity, Providence continues to welcome immigrants from across the globe: men and women who have left an indelible, flavorful mark on the local food scene. Add to this the influence of the world's largest culinary arts school, Johnson & Wales University, and it's not surprising that the *Wall Street Journal* recently chose Providence as the only US city in its list of Top Ten Emerging Tourist Destinations.

From fresh pasta and seafood creations at one of the many traditional Italian restaurants on historic Federal Hill to the premium cuts available at several renowned steak houses throughout the Downcity District, and an amazing variety of Latino and Southeast Asian offerings on the West End and South Side neighborhoods, Providence offers a unique culinary experience for every taste.

Whether you are a native Rhode Islander or simply visiting Providence for business or pleasure, this in-depth guide, written by two of New England's most respected food writers, Deborah Moxham and John Schenck, is a must read. More than just a restaurant guide, this book offers readers a comprehensive guide to Providence's extraordinary culinary culture and a fresh perspective on the worldwide influences, from Naples to Phnom Penh, that make our city so unique and appealing.

I invite you to enjoy *The Providence Guide: 91 Best Restaurants*. It is, without a doubt, the most comprehensive and entertaining guide to culinary excellence in the city of Providence.

Regards,

David N. Cicilline
Mayor of the City of Providence

A few other cities and towns the size of Providence perhaps offer as much good eating as here, but they're probably in Tuscany. And even in Tuscany, your options are limited! There, the restaurants are obviously mostly Italian (not at all a bad thing), whereas here there's a restaurant for every craving.

When we decided to write a restaurant guide to Providence, we did so with the enthusiasm of travelers beginning an exciting journey. Debby is a longtime Providence resident who knows the food scene here inside and out, and John is a native New Yorker who has gotten over his Gothamite chauvinism.

Over the course of a year or so, we've eaten in just about every place in town that calls itself a restaurant. In this guide, we have focused on places where we knew, or at least had heard, that the food is good, and where we could sit down to eat. Providence is home to a number of establishments where you eat on the run, and for the most part we've left those out. We both believe that a good meal, while not necessarily fancy or pricey, does need to be lingered over long enough to appreciate its flavors and presentation. A meal should be a relaxing break, not a pit stop.

A remarkable spectrum of restaurants fits that bill, from the high end – landmarks like Al Forno – to affordable little storefronts like Pho Paradise and Chapinlandia where dedicated ethnic chefs prepare dishes that we'd never tried before and that entice us to return again and again. We hope that you, our readers, are seized with the spirit of discovery and will explore some of these unfamiliar cuisines, because it is this diversity that really sets

Providence apart. Here, in a little city of 176,000, you can find the cooking of, yes, America, France and Italy, but also of Argentina, Guatemala, Cambodia, Korea, Viet Nam, Mexico, Japan, China, India and Thailand. When we write about restaurants, we are, of course, subjective. We might go into one restaurant that we may have once considered marginal and yet feel so sheltered and pampered that it soars to the top of the list. We have tried to be sincere in our judgments and have compiled a list of restaurants that *you* can consider. We think every restaurant on this list warrants your attention, and we leave the rest up to your evaluation. Perhaps, the wait staff may be off their game the night you go, or the line chef may be home sick, but on the other hand, it might just be a night when everything exceeds expectation.

We do believe all the establishments in this book are serious places, making a concerted effort to gain your loyalty and satisfaction. We appreciate how much work goes into that effort, how expensive ingredients have become, and how difficult it is for a much praised place to maintain the perfect reputation every single night. And although the number of patrons has not grown in Providence, the number of restaurants has increased multifold. We do love our restaurants and are sympathetic to their challenges and grateful for their successes.

We recommend every restaurant here. We have our favorites (list on p. 111), and when we have a peeve, we'll let you know about it. But it is a remarkable fact that we can eagerly advise you to try any of the 91 restaurants reviewed here. There is, as the saying goes, strength in diversity, and a lot of good eating, too.

THE RESTAURANTS

1. Agora

The Westin Providence (Downcity)
1 W. Exchange Street
Providence, RI 02903
401-598-8011
Breakfast, Lunch, Dinner daily
Brunch on Sunday
Reservations
$$$-$$$$

After you've ascended the long escalator from the Westin Hotel lobby and entered Agora's roomy and comfortable confines, you still know you're in a hotel restaurant. First, the tables are widely spaced, telling you that the hotel calls the shots, not some nervous chef with an overzealous accountant. Then there's the music: it's good old-fashioned hotel elevator music, almost below the level of audibility, but it still fills the room with a kind of aural tapioca. Although it is comforting, you could do without it.

Menu offerings are not surprising but are well prepared and attractively presented. The strong suit is seafood. Maine lobster is almost always available. At lunch Agora serves an almost-perfect lobster roll with chive mayonnaise ($14.00). It comes on a brioche, which you may appreciate as an elegant upgrade. Perhaps you will pine for the classic buttered, grilled New England hot dog roll, which in our view is perfection. You may be tempted by the thin-crust Roma pizza ($11.00), and if you are, give in. It is a 12" disc of just crispy enough grilled dough topped with three cheeses (parmigiano, mozzarella and fontina) plus wild mushrooms, peppers and tomato. It is a white pizza without a drop of red sauce, and it tastes almost truffly from the mushrooms and cheese. Sunday Brunch includes a full buffet of tempting eggs, meats, an omelet station and a lovely assortment of pastries. Highly recommended.

It's hard to categorize Agora because although the food is good and the setting attractive, it is all a bit generic. It is definitely ideal for a business lunch, perhaps, because the table spacing insures privacy, and that works equally well for an intimate dinner date. You will select your wine from a fine list. Nothing about the restaurant will embarrass you, but there is something in its personality that could use a little zing. Still, if you're at or near the Westin or the Convention Center or shopping at Providence Place, or if your guests are staying at the hotel, it is a top-notch option.

2. Al Forno

577 South Main Street (Fox Point)
Providence, RI 02903
401-273-9760
www.alforno.com
Dinner Tuesday – Saturday
$$$-$$$$

Many of us remember going to Al Forno when it had just opened up as a tiny six-table restaurant. That was 25 years ago, and it was unquestionably the most exciting restaurant in Providence. Al Forno is Providence's most famous restaurant, filled with patrons from all over the region who have heard or read about it. Frequent visitors to Providence make Al Forno their first choice, and for good reason. George Germon and Johanne Killeen have created and sustained an incomparable restaurant.

Not only is the food superb, but also the artistic hand of George is evident in the color palette, in the material on the floors and the exquisite outdoor garden which transports you to Provence on summer evenings. At the top of the stairs, Kyle is at the bar, welcoming old friends and making new ones, as he mixes some of the best cocktails in town. When you select your meal from the heavenly menu, you will dine on pastas and grilled specialties which are brilliantly and aggressively flavorful – this is not food for the timid of palate. The pizzas have been celebrated in major magazines and newspapers; Johanne and George have garnered a superb national reputation, and their cookbooks invite you to share their recipes.

The dessert selection is dramatic, elegant and tempting, and your server will present special choices as you order your dinner. George and Johanne have worked hard for their success, and they have held onto it because of their insistence on excellence. Yes, it's a special occasion restaurant: too pricey for frequent dining, and yet you know that it will always deliver. On the other hand, we must note that it's hard to plan for a special occasion when you can't lock in a reservation, something that always makes us feel the diner is secondary in the formula.

At press time, Johanne and George were preparing to open a new restaurant called Tini. And tiny it will be in - a 450 square foot space on Washington Street. The plan is that everything will be small--plates, table glasses, silverware - but not flavors. Think tapas style without being Spanish. The wine glass, however, is not downsized. About 30 boutique wines will be available. All seating will surround a u-shaped white marble bar.

3. Andreas Restaurant

268 Thayer Street (College Hill)
Providence, RI 02906
401-331-7879
www.andreasri.com
Lunch, Dinner daily
Brunch Saturday and Sunday
$$

Andreas is a rather gussied-up version of the classic Greek-American restaurant. You dine in a welcoming and modern setting which complements the traditional food. Its location, right on the corner of Thayer and Meeting Streets attracts the Brown and East Side communities, and its food and reasonable prices insure returning patrons.

You will find virtually all the classic dishes of the Greek-American repertoire on the menu. If you begin with a bowl of avgolemono soup, you won't be disappointed; it's rich and chickeny, with a distinct lemon tang. Chunks of white meat chicken float in it, and flecks of fresh parsley dress up the dish and add a fresh taste. It is both satisfying and reasonably priced at just $3 a bowl.

Souvlaki ($8) is about the messiest sandwich on the planet, but once you resign yourself to use at least six napkins or to eat it with implements, you should be happy. The big pieces of marinated lamb are cooked to order, so you can have yours medium-rare; the meat rests in the grilled pita along with a tzatziki sauce of tangy yogurt, garlic and cucumber, plus peppers and onions. It comes with fries or a Greek salad. The fries are good, but it's the salad, dressed with a tasty feta vinaigrette, that truly complements the rich and gooey sandwich.

At dinner, Andreas offers standard steak, chop, and seafood fare, but also kabobs, pastitsio, moussaka, and lemon oregano lamb chops, all of which are classically Greek and perfectly seasoned. Greek dinner specialties run from about $14 to $18. A surprisingly ambitious wine list represents numerous Greek vintages. Greek wine was once dominated by an alarming white, retsina, which tastes mostly of pine needles. Now you can choose from a variety of interesting Greek estate-bottled reds and whites. One of them would surely complete your meal.

In the summer you can dine outdoors at Andreas and watch the diverse spectrum of people stroll up and down Thayer Street and even see the young people come and go from Johnny Rocket's across the street. On a warm evening, as you mop up the last of your moussaka and think about another glass of Plages Kmidion, you can almost imagine that the Aegean is just steps away.

4. Angelo's Civita Farnese

141 Atwells Avenue (Federal Hill)
Providence, RI 02903
401-621-8171
www.angelosonthehill.com
Lunch, Dinner daily
Reservations dinner only
$$

Even if we didn't want to include Angelo's in our list, we would defer to the tremendous clientele that has kept this place in business for 84 years. So many places come and go, but Angelo's obviously delivers what a loyal, as well as ever-replenishing, stock of diners seeks. It's the FOOD – straightforward, good, honest well prepared Italian food – not haute cuisine that will satisfy you. The surroundings are a bonus.

If you're Italian-American, this is what you probably grew up on: pastine (white or red); escarole and bean soup; spaghetti aglio e olio; eggplant parmigiana; linguine with clams; braciole, tripe, pasta fagiole. And, of course, fried calamari and fried smelts.

Angelo's is a welcoming, good-looking place. It has been in the heart of Atwells Avenue since 1924 and has obviously had a couple of face-lifts so that it now has a warm, contemporary, men's grill kind of look. There's an elevated track above the central bar and sometimes a little train tootles along the rails. Often at lunchtime a couple of older Atwellians work their way through a plate of pasta and a long-neck. It couldn't feel more comfortable for them, and for us, as well as for the bankers, journalists and politicians who frequent their beloved Angelo's.

The food (we almost said "cuisine") is unsurprising, unless you count the tripe, which is perfectly prepared. That's a tricky dish, tripe. This version was tender and flavorful in a sturdy tomato sauce ($5.60). A plate of "homemade" aglio e oglio turned out to be perfect fettucine, just a few seconds past al dente, with a quite emphatic oil and garlic bath coating every slippery strand ($8.30). Regular, i.e., non-homemade, aglio e olio is $6.75, and in that selection, you get spaghetti. Angelo's has three Chiantis by the glass, two at $4.75, plus other reasonably priced offerings.

There is nothing trendy about Angelo's. It's the kind of spot you're happy to be near when you're hungry and have a craving for Italian comfort food served in a place that makes no demands except that you relax and enjoy your meal. So – mangia.

5. Angkor

333 Wickenden Street (Fox Point)
Providence RI 02906
401-383-2227
Lunch, Dinner Monday-Saturday
Reservations
$$

Angkor is a charming genial spot that serves celestial Cambodian food. We had several dishes at Angkor that we have never had before, each of which introduced us to new flavors and textures. The owners explained that Cambodian food most resembles Thai in the use of coconut milk and lemongrass, but it certainly has its own distinctive flavor. A dish called Natang consisted of six crispy rice crackers and a warm bowl of ground pork cooked in coconut milk with fragrant spices and cilantro. The crunch of the crackers under the succulent pork was an exciting surprise. Other appetizers include chive dumplings, scallion pancakes, and a soup called Nam Yaa. The Nam Yaa is described as a medicine soup, good for the sinuses, but indeed it is a sweet and spicy broth flecked with lemongrass, ginger, galangal, kaffir lime leaves and chicken or shrimp. Many of the dishes at Angkor are new to us, like Rice Mitapheap, which is served with garlic, rice, lettuce, tomatoes and pickle salad, and Street Noodles, composed of marinated meats stir-fried with rice noodles and assorted vegetables, eggs, curry and coconut sauce.

There is a moving story that goes with Angkor, which explains the culinary success of the restaurant. The special recipes were passed down to a woman named Bopha Kem, from an aunt who was a personal chef for the Cambodian royal family. Through her interest in cooking, which she learned from her aunt, Bopha was deemed worthy of receiving the recipes. Bopha smuggled her book of recipes out of Cambodia during the Khmer Rouge Civil War, into the United States. How lucky we are that Bopha is cooking in the kitchen, along with her daughter and son-in-law, who own Angkor.

Angkor is well worth a visit for its moderate prices and lovely service. More importantly, however, is the opportunity to taste authentic food prepared at its best.

6. Bacaro

262 South Water Street (Fox Point)
Providence, RI 02903
401-751-3700
www.bacarorestaurant.net
Dinner Tuesday - Saturday
Reservations 6 or more
$$$$

After cooking at Al Forno for nearly a dozen years, Chef Brian Kingsford recently opened his own spot. Bacaro is housed in a handsome two-story restaurant on the riverbank. Kingsford offers the same world class thin-crusted grilled pizza as Al Forno; the differences are in the toppings rather than in the texture and the deliciousness. Some of the same sinful and sensational baked pastas appear on the menu. We like the gratin of pasta with mushrooms and fresh tomatoes. When seated, you will receive a Salumeria menu; Kingsford offers outstanding salumeria, allowing you to create a customized antipasto. Not only does the salumeria offer imported cured meats and cheeses, but it also includes foie gras on crostini with sweet fig jam. We ordered extensively from the salumeria and nibbled on cippoline agro dolce, arancini and anchovy and fried sage sandwiches. Our group of six argued over who had the best entrée, and some of the favorites were Crispy Chicken over buttered noodles, a Roast Haddock with cardoon gratin, and pan roasted hot Italian sausages in vinegar on grilled polenta.

Bacaro offers artisanal food, with the focus on fresh local seafood and produce and fine imported items. Chef Brian obviously knows his craft and has earned a loyal following over the years. We wish Bacaro would take reservations so that we could count on spending an evening there from time to time, but as it stands, you need a group of six or more to plan your evening. Nonetheless, Bacaro has found its niche in the Providence restaurant scene, and if we have to resign ourselves to weeknight visits when the crowds are thinner, then so be it. We will frequent Bacaro for the chef's craft and attention to detail.

7. Blaze

272 Thayer Street (College Hill) and
776 Hope Street (Hope Street)
Providence, RI 02906
401-490-2128 (College Hill)
401-277-2529 (Hope Street)
www.blazeeastside.com
Lunch, Dinner Tuesday – Saturday
Hope Street serves dinner on Sunday
Reservations
$$

Blaze on Hope Street opened to great acclaim in 2005. Its success on the East Side inspired its owners to ignite another slightly more casual Blaze on Thayer Street. The idea is the same – reasonably priced "American Fusion Cuisine" in a casual and friendly atmosphere. The Thayer Street restaurant is spacious, with about 90 seats, including 20 or so in the attractive bar area. The menu offers something for just about everyone, with salads, burgers, wraps and pizzas leading the lunch menu, and mains (or "Big Bites") on the dinner menu ranging from a 14-oz. pork chop to wild mushroom ravioli, St. Louis style spareribs, and Cape Verde pork and littlenecks. The most expensive menu entrée is the black pepper beef tenderloin at $20.95, a dish that made many friends at Blaze on Hope Street. No doubt it will be just as popular on Thayer, in the center of the student universe, especially when Mom and Dad are treating.

Pay special attention to the Blaze BBQ burger, a hefty - but not obscenely so - patty on a Kaiser roll with cheddar cheese, bacon and bbq sauce topped with French-fried onion rings. The burger is perfectly charred and the sauce has some real zip. Pizzas are more or less trapezoidal, with a very thin, nicely blackened-around-the-edges crust and an intriguing choice of toppings, ranging from a traditional (and scrumptious) margarita to the "hot as a mutha" pizza, with its "XXX spice-rubbed crust."

Wines by the glass are reasonably priced, mostly in the $5 - $8 range. The choices are interesting, many from less-predictable sources than your average pizza-and-wrap joint.

Of the two, Blaze on Hope Street is more focused on cuisine. Despite its Joe College setting and informal vibe, Blaze on Thayer is a serious restaurant with honestly tasty food and a great attitude. And there is bound to be something on the welcoming, varied menu that will speak your language. Maybe the chocolate mousse banana split cake with caramel and walnuts? You can bring the whole darn gateau home with you for just $34.55.

8. Blue Grotto

21 Atwells Avenue (Federal Hill)
Providence RI 02903
401-272-9030
www.bluegrottorestaurant.com
Lunch Monday-Friday
Dinner nightly
Reservations
$$$

When the Blue Grotto opened in 1980, it was about the hottest place on the hill. Now it has new owners and the blue tuxedoed waiters have gone the way of the ornate lighting fixtures. The atmosphere is now distinctly more informal. The food, still classic Italian, is well prepared and reasonably priced.

The lunch menu offers a hearty portobella mushroom stuffed with red peppers and romano cheese, roasted and drizzled with truffle oil. An Insalata Siciliana of baby arugula, escarole, grilled corn, scallion, radish, radicchio, and orange wedges dressed in lemon pepper vinaigrette was both unusual and delicious for $6. Our favorite sandwich was the PLT – pancetta, lettuce and tomato with basil mayonnaise on toasted ciabatta bread. At dinner, Blue Grotto has an excellent Osso Buco for $24, and offers interesting options like a slow-roasted rabbit stew or a risotto with scallops, shrimp, mussels and baby squid. Veal Saltimbocca and Chicken Parmigiana are among the de rigueur classic Italian dishes available.

The décor at Blue Grotto leaves a bit to be desired, more resembling a Holiday Inn than an old world Italian ristorante. The food is worth a visit, and with 200 seats you can probably get in when some of the smaller Hill restaurants are full. There are 300 bottles on the wine list and 35 options by the glass; a glass will run you anywhere from $6 to $16.

9. Bob & Timmy's

32 Spruce Street (Federal Hill)
Providence RI 02903
401-453-2221
Lunch, Dinner daily
$

On a block of Spruce Street near Dean, Bob & Timmy's does food the old-fashioned way, serving grilled pizza with a variety of toppings. In fact, Bob & Timmy's bills itself as "the original wood-grilled pizza on the Hill." When you enter, it's darkish in a comforting corner tavern kind of way. A couple of neon beer signs glimmer in the window, and a couple of guys nurse their drinks at the cozy wood bar. Soups are good, especially the minestrone. But if you're a regular, you know what to order. If this is your first visit, go directly to the Grille Classic: wild mushrooms, grilled onions, pepperoni, parmesan and romano cheeses, and marinara sauce. The pies are all 14 inches, and the crust is thin and crisp with its savory, balanced mix of ingredients on top will not stuff you.

Bob & Timmy's has a full menu so if you're not in the mood for pizza, you can select from a surprising number of non-pizza choices. But pizza, wood-grilled, is really the point.

10. Bravo Brasserie

123 Empire Street (Downcity)
Providence, RI 02903
401-490-5112
www.bravobrasserie.com
Lunch, Dinner daily
Brunch on weekends
$$ -$$$

Bravo has many pluses, starting with an appealing menu and interesting, reasonably priced wines. It show up on practically everyone's top ten list. There's a welcoming bar up front and a classic bistro dining room with dark red leather banquettes and wood tables. The service is friendly and attentive, and the food is, by and large, delicious. That menu doesn't hold any big surprises, unless you call a "Foie Gras PB&J" appetizer a surprise, which we guess we'd have to say we do. The sesame-infused tuna tartare appetizer comes with little pita chips for scooping and a tasty sliced cucumber salad. Mainly the selections run to bistro favorites like moules, filet au poivre, half roast chicken, steak frites, mac & cheese, and daily specials that go from coq au vin to prime rib. On a recent visit, the filet au poivre was perfectly cooked but lacked any discernable poivre. Many main courses come with fries, which are delicious. Salads are huge – they really are full meals – made with top-notch ingredients and nicely dressed, too. Excellent burgers and sandwiches are always available. Bravo does not feature a lengthy dessert list, but it does offer a perfectly-crusted crème brulée and a nice flourless chocolate cake along with a cheese plate, sorbets and ice creams.

Located right across the street from the Trinity Repertory Company, Bravo is perfect for pre- or post-theater dining – but if you go after the play starts, the place will have calmed down and you can linger a bit over your meal. You should do that.

11. Broadway Bistro

205 Broadway (Federal Hill)
Providence RI 02903
401-331-2450
Lunch, Dinner nightly
Reservations - 6 or more
$$

This little restaurant opened up just before we went to press. We're delighted at this addition to the Providence dining scene. Broadway Bistro is a cozy, charming boite on the corner of Broadway and Pallas Street. There are just enough seats for about thirty at the tables and another nine at the bar. The room is red with an olive green panel over the black bar, and the white cloth-topped tables sport various shades of red in their underskirts. An eclectic variety of artwork adds warmth to the ambience.

Owner-chef Pat Lowney has cooked at a number of high-end places, and has clearly honed his own skills. He offers a menu with enough of a twist to make it interesting and enough of the classics to keep us happy. Come in at lunch for dishes like a "Salad on Steak" for $9.00, featuring a 4 ounce hanger steak with fresh greens bathed in sage vinaigrette, complemented by a gooey chewy blue cheese fritter. The combination of textures and flavors works together in a very satisfying way. The steak is cooked exactly right; the salad is fresh and herby, and the fritter a little bit decadent. A pork and beans stew in a thyme-flavored broth is hearty and comforting. The cannellini beans are perfect – not mealy, not hard, and spiked by spicy chourico. At only $5.00, it might be the best deal in Providence for lunch.

At dinner you'll find many of the same dishes along with some tempting additions. An appetizer of braised beef cheeks with carrot mash, parsley and fried fennel is $8.00, as are the shrimp dumplings with port beurre blanc, lettuce and prosciutto. The peppercorn crusted tuna with zucchini spears, pesto, tomato, kalamata vinaigrette is the highest priced dinner item at $20 and the lamb shank shepherd's pie is $15.

Wines by the glass are in the seven dollar range. The full wine list, while not vast, includes many intriguing boutique wine and unconventional choices from artisanal sources. The service is attentive, and the atmosphere is inviting. Best of all the food is terrific and the prices are just right.

12. Café Nuovo

1 Citizens Plaza (Downcity)
Providence RI 02903
401- 421-2525
www.cafenuovo.com
Lunch Monday –Friday
Dinner nightly
Reservations
$$$$

You need to book six weeks in advance to have dinner at Café Nuovo on a WaterFire night. It is indisputably the prime site for riverside dining. The Café dining room sits against the brick walkway that banks the river, and when the weather is warm enough, dining al fresco provides the ultimate experience. What a scene! What a happy experience as you dine in the midst of a great crowd, who hear the sound of crackling firewood, catch the aroma of that special wood, see the hundreds of passers-by, and view the black clad Waterfire volunteers stocking the pyres. That would be enough for anyone, even if they served wieners. But they don't.

Under the careful direction of Executive Chef Tim Kelly, Café Nuovo prepares some of the fanciest food in town. Even the breadbasket you get at the beginning of the meal is worth mentioning. The focaccia is scented with fennel and has a crisp crust; the Italian bread is chewy and yeasty. The eclectic menu offers steaks and seafood and lovely Italian fare like stuffed rigatoni saltimbocca: oversized rigatoni filled with portabella, prosciutto di Parma, crimini mushrooms and veal in a red wine. But there's much more. Sous-Chef Manuel Ojeda lends an exciting Latin twist to the menu, offering dishes like a steak burrito, featuring avocado mousse and pico de gallo that sings with cilantro. Some of the other notable and popular dishes include risotto with Bomster sea scallops on a bed of risotto spiked with preserved lemon, parmigiana, olive oil and Pinot Noir syrup, In addition you may choose fried spaghetti with shrimp scampi, or Amarillo chicken wrap. The desserts are gloriously fashioned; our favorite is the decadent chocolate mousse cake with its towering spun sugar and crisp wafers. Each dessert looks more beautiful than the last.

Owner Dimitri Kritikos has run Café Nuovo since its inception, and he has achieved greatness in cuisine, presentation, attention to detail, and, not to be even slightly forgotten, tremendous service. This special occasion restaurant offers specialties that are not just good, they are presented as works of art. The waitstaff is informed, and unintrusive, yet very helpful.

Café Nuovo is more expensive than many places, but then it provides more. The view is to die for. It is a lovely place for lunch when you want to treat yourself well. A typical luncheon entrée is about $14.00. For dinner, you can expect your entrée to cost around $30; appetizers at dinner time are about $11. Wines by the glass run between $8 and $12. The wine list is pricey, but impressive.

13. Caffe Dolce Vita

59 DePasquale Plaza (Federal Hill)
Providence, RI 02903
401-331-8240
www.caffedolcevita.com
Breakfast, lunch, dinner daily
Brunch on weekends
Reservations
$$

Smack dab in the middle of De Pasquale Plaza, Caffe Dolce Vita is a great spot for breakfast, lunch or dinner. It has enjoyed tremendous popularity every summer. Sit outside and you get a birdseye view of opera, cabaret singers, or simply passersby. The good food is appealing all year round and all day long. Caffe Dolce Vita is open from 8 a.m. until 1 a.m. the following morning, so if you have a hankering for a light snack at any hour, you can order from the appetizer list. Arancini di Riso, a dish of two crisp risotto croquettes filled with ground veal, vegetables, and parmigiana and topped with marinara sauce, makes a comforting and satisfying lunch or mid-afternoon pick me up. Eggplant rollatini is another tempting choice. Salads are very good, especially Elaine Scampoli's, with spring greens, crumbled gorgonzola, dried cherries, candied walnuts and a honey peppercorn dressing. The menu offers paninis and pastas and serious dinner entrees like veal or chicken marsala, grilled salmon, and eggplant parmigiana. Owner Gianfranco Marocco, who owns the adjoining hotel, the Villa Dolce Vita, as well as Geppetto's and Mediterraneo, is never far away, regularly checking out his place to enforce his high standards. We didn't try it, but are told the brunch menu is extremely popular and with offerings like French Toast Napoleon and Eggs Benedict, the place is usually packed.

Day or night, it seems there is a hot bar scene as well. Caffe Dolce Vita is casual, attractive and a good option for a cocktail or any number of meals.

14. Camille's

71 Bradford Street (Federal Hill)
Providence, RI 02903
401-751-4812
Lunch Monday – Friday
Dinner Monday-Saturday
www.camillesonthehill.com
Reservations
$$$

Executive Chef John Granata has retained the old-fashioned Italian ambience and food at Camille's. A local dining landmark since 1914, Camille's was originally located right on Atwells Avenue, but moved in 1919 to an old mansion at 71 Bradford Street, one door in from Atwells. The cuisine is classic mainstream Italian, served in a dim but eclectically sumptuous environment where the food is the star. If you're looking for a place to take visitors who want the full Federal Hill experience with elegance as well as authenticity, Camille's will more than fill the bill.

When you enter the dining room, you see nicely spaced tables, elegantly set. You'll get a bread basket and a beaker of extra-virgin olive oil for your table and even though you're going to get plenty of food, definitely grab a piece of the multigrain bread and dip it in the oil. The bread is exceptional, crisp-crusted and hearty, and great when enriched by the fruity oil. The menu, especially at dinner, is comprehensive and appealing, with a full array of antipasti, pastas, seafood, salads, chicken, veal and steak dishes. If you start with clams oreganata ($10), for example, you'll get six cherrystones, covered with an herby breadcrumb topping. The crumbs are nicely browned and the clams are hot but still sweet, tender and juicy. Nothing worse than an overcooked baked clam, and unfortunately nothing more common. Not here…ever! The clams are perfect at Camille's.

Pastas ("Farinaci" on the dinner menu, plain old pasta at lunch) range from tagliatelle Bolognese to spaghetti with sausage or meatballs to gnocchi to capellini aglio e olio. The Bolognese is especially noteworthy. At Camille's, Chef Granata prepares this sauce with three meats (beef, pork and veal), and its long simmering produces a thick and rich coating which permeates each strand of the al dente tagliatelle. It's a big portion, and at $22 at dinner, it's not inexpensive, but it will make you happy.

Camille's prides itself on its prime beef. Bistecca alla Mama con Funghi (sirloin with garlic butter and mushrooms) is a pricey

$42, as are the other sirloin offerings. Filet mignon with Barolo is a relative bargain at $39. Veal Milanese is another $42 option, but the ingredients and preparation are first-rate. The wine list is wide-ranging and wines by the glass, not necessarily all Italian, are in the $9 range.

Camille's has been cooking for Providence for almost a century. Atmosphere, service, and above all good food, carefully prepared and presented, explain its longevity. It will probably still be good for a visit sometime in the 22nd century.

15. Capital Grille

1 Union Station (Downcity)
Providence RI 02903
401-521-5600
www.thecapitalgrille.com
Lunch Monday-Friday
Dinner nightly
Reservations
$$$$

The Capital Grille, opened in 1992, was the first really big-time steakhouse in town, and now it has not only grown to the point where it has branches in major cities, but also it has attracted imitators right at home. However, it is the steakhouse that still draws repeat and new diners to its handsome headquarters in the Union Station area, with dry-aged steaks and a Webster's Unabridged-style wine list. Its "we aim-to-please" service and a location that's perfect for business lunches as well as for Big Nights Out add to its success.

The menu does not break any new ground, and you wouldn't want a steakhouse to do that anyway. What you will find among the appetizers, which include caviar at dinner, is pan-fried calamari with hot cherry peppers. Clearly, although this restaurant has become a chain, The Capital Grille knows its Rhode Islanders and their roots. The steaks are dry-aged on the premises, which you can view in a large case by the bar. They're beefy, tender and full of that mineral zing that only dry-aging lends to beef. The menu includes seafood options as well, lobsters, swordfish, shrimp are fresh and tempting, and pasta and vegetarian choices will satisfy those who do not eat meat.

Everything about The Capital Grill is professional. The staff knows how to please its diners, from the bar to the kitchen to the dining room. The food is exactly as described, the wine well-chosen and fairly priced for the most part. The private dining room is secluded but not isolated, and the rest rooms are tucked away and attractive. If you like creative cuisine, Providence has many options for you. But if you're in the mood for red meat, this Rhode Island original is still one of the very best choices in town.

16. Capriccio

2 Pine St (Downcity)
Providence, RI 02903
401-421-1320
www.capriccio.com
Lunch Monday-Friday
Dinner nightly
Reservations
$$$$

The ladies in their furs stand outside of Capriccio, waiting for their cars. On a cold and blustery Providence winter evening, they clutch doggie-bag containers as wind and sleet swirl around them. They look extremely happy. One of them says, "Great food AND service!" as we pass by on our way into the entrance door held by the valet.

Capriccio is a throwback, but not like the old-school Italian places on Federal Hill with their veal and eggplant parmigiana. Capriccio is a throwback to a kind of restaurant that is virtually extinct, the kind of place you might remember visiting with your parents for a really, really big event sometime around the inauguration of JFK in 1961. It's the kind of place where butter and cream are deployed in prodigious quantities and where the art of flambéing is not just practiced, but perfected. It is the kind of place where you'll savor tastes and textures you thought you'd forgotten, but they were in your memory all along, and you're deeply grateful that they've been revived.

When you walk down the stairs into Capriccio's grotto-like subterranean space, you enter a sybaritic world. You are seated in throne-like chairs and given atlas-sized menus bound in rrreeech Correenthian leatherrr, or a substance very similar. Your fellow diners are rather senior for the most part, and they are enjoying themselves enormously. Many of them seem to be on very friendly terms with the waiters, whether from long acquaintance or simple bonhomie.

Your waiter recites the specials, takes drink orders, and leaves you to consider your options. They are numerous. Among the appetizers are classics like shrimp cocktail ($ market), prosciutto and melon ($12.95), and clams casino (a/k/a "Clams Capriccio," $12.95). They are all first-rate. A wonderful first course is Straciatella alla Romano, chicken broth with egg white and spinach, dressed with freshly grated Parmigiano ($5.50). It's a special, but if it is the soup di giorno when you visit, do order it. It's warming and not heavy, and considering what lies ahead, you may want to enjoy its delicate flavor.

Main dishes at Capriccio include offerings that make you realize how good butter makes everything taste – and how, if you add enough cream to the butter, it tastes even better. Dover sole meunière ($mkt) is presented and filleted tableside. It is succulent, the fish itself tasting as if it had swum in butter all its life and the lemon butter sauce does nothing to dispel this impression. Fettucine Alfredo ($21.95), a dish once wildly popular that has all but disappeared from menus, is tossed in egg, butter and cream, then showered with Parmigiana. The pasta is perfectly al dente, the sauce is rich without being gluey. Now you remember why it was so popular, but was it ever this good? Tenderloin Diane, a flattened filet mignon flambéed with mushrooms, shallots and brandy ($32.95) is both floor show and main dish. It's prepared on a tableside trolley, so you really see the creation of your dish as your server slathers the meat with Dijon mustard, sautés shallots and ignites the steak with brandy that flares up to the ceiling with a whoosh just before he finishes the tender steak with cream. Extremely exciting.

The wine list is especially strong in Italian vintages, with several Chianti Classicos in the $40-$60 range and Brunellos and Barolos at higher tariffs. Overall the list is wide-ranging and well-chosen.

Desserts include crepes with or without seasonal berries. The crepes are, of course, flambéed tableside, in case you haven't had enough pyrotechnics yet, and taste wonderful.

You haven't had a meal like this in decades. This kind of theatrical presentation is uncommon today. See what you've been missing? The only thing that isn't old-school about Capriccio is the prices, which are high, but you'll get your money's worth. As the lady in the fur said, "great food AND service." Plus, you will probably be clutching a doggie bag with the food you were unable to finish tonight, so you have a treat to look forward to tomorrow.

17. Casa Christine

123 Spruce Street (Federal Hill)
Providence, RI 02903
401-453-6255
Lunch, dinner Tuesday - Saturday
BYOB, no credit cards
Reservations
$$

Casa Christine might be the most contrary little spot on our list. Tucked behind the fancier places on Atwells Avenue, it serves authentic Italian cuisine in an old house on Spruce Street. Menus hang on white erasable boards and a couple of vintage signs hang on the walls. Lighting is not exactly designed to enhance your tan. But there's an authentic feeling of time and place, perhaps during the Eisenhower administration, but emphatically it is a Federal Hill spot. It has crazy hours, takes no credit cards, and serves no liquor. There is nothing fancy in the decor, but the ambrosial cuisine that emerges from the kitchen more than explains why Casa Christine has enjoyed a strong following for 18 years. White beans bathed in olive oil and garlic, topped with tomato and soppressata, and served on garlic bread is as rustic and earthy a dish as the chicken francese is a delicate one. The chicken is lightly coated in an egg batter and cooked in butter with a lemon accent. The kitchen eschews garnishes, so every dish arrives just the way we all did once, naked and unadorned and pure. A daily menu includes about thirty choices including appetizers like littlenecks in white wine and entrees such as chicken arrabbiata, eggplant parmigiana or steak pizzaiola.

Chef owner Bill Calise is the genius at the stove and also, the decider. Calise sets the puzzling hours: lunch until 1:15 when the doors are locked and reopens in the late afternoon for dinner. They lock again at 7:30. As for Christine herself, she has been known to haul out the Hoover and start vacuuming the dining room before the diners have had dessert. So you kind of have to know the food is great so that you can adapt to the owners' proclivities.

Casa Christine does take reservations and the word is you'll need them, since regulars show up at four for dinner. The atmosphere is convivial. Tony Bennett and Frank Sinatra provide the music, and the prices are reasonable. Bring your own Chianti and Prosecco and pay a one time $5.00 charge for wine opening. Then sit back and let the garlic aroma waft into your nostrils and the seductive flavors tickle your tastebuds, and figure out when you want to return. Just lift your feet when the vacuum comes by.

18. Cassarino's

177 Atwells Avenue (Federal Hill)
Providence RI 02903
401-751-1333
www.cassarinosri.com
Lunch Monday-Friday
Dinner Monday-Saturday
Reservations
$$

Cassarino's, another old timer on Federal Hill, is an attractive eatery because of its surroundings, its food, its prices and its fine service. It offers a wide range of reasonably priced classic Southern Italian food, along with options like filet mignon and mashed potatoes. We had dinner in a cozy booth in the back room one winter night, where we could hear ourselves talk despite a happy, filled dining room. We looked out on the front room with its warm wood paneling and twinkling Christmas lights. Had it been summer, we would have been happy to be sitting by the open French doors in that room, watching the hustle and bustle of Atwells Avenue. Our waitress, who has worked at Cassarino's for four years, gave us informed opinions on the menu, which has some longstanding offerings. The warm goat cheese bubbling in marinara sauce surrounded by garlic bread was a terrific choice, although it might as well have been dinner, given the generous size. In fact, all the meals were giant sized for Little Rhodies, and each of us left most of the meal on the plate, because it simply was too much. But it was good: the arrabbiata with sausage was as spicy as described; the filet was cooked to perfection. The pollo con broccoli rabe was a flavorful dish of chicken and sausage with rabe, red peppers and prosciutto in a garlic and olive sauce served over penne and finished with gorgonzola cheese.

The dessert list features molten lava cake, crème brulée and tiramisu along with other choices. The wine list stretches over three pages of reds, whites and champagnes and includes eighteen selections by the glass with an average price of $6.50.

A year ago, longtime employees Tyler Baron and Steve Renzi bought Cassarino's from Richard Cassarino, but they held fast to the successful formula the restaurant has followed. The popularity of Cassarino's continues. In the summer when Federal Hill stages its stroll and restaurants prepare a tasting, Cassarino's has captured First Prize for the past three years.

19. CAV

14 Imperial Place (Downcity)
Providence RI 02903
401-751-9164
www.cavrestaurant.com
Lunch, Dinner Monday - Saturday
Brunch on weekends
Reservations
$$$

Cav is unlike any other place in Providence; it's probably unlike any place anywhere. It is the personal triumph of its owner, Sylvia Moubayed, who started it as a coffee house (CAV is an acronym for coffee, antiques and victuals), and it has evolved into a sophisticated and enchanting restaurant with absolutely top quality fare. The warm and glittering space has many hanging crystal chandeliers lighting up the brick walls which are covered with African and Asian art. Each table is set with a colorful Kilim carpet topped with glass; the chairs, which must be the most comfortable restaurant chairs in the world, are upholstered Biedermeiers, elegant and classic. Moubayed's influence is so pervasive, from the décor to the food and service, that it is unimaginable that Cav could ever be replicated without her. Indeed, a national survey for *Details* magazine selected Cav as "one of the 300 most unique places in the United States."

But onto the food, which Moubayed supervises proudly. It is no wonder that Cav has won dozens of awards and been featured in many magazines including *Architectural Digest* and *Bon Appetit*. It is difficult to choose among appetizers like a pistachio crusted crabcake with Sriracha aioli and lotus root, fois gras served on grilled brioche with a warm apple and beet salad in a toasted fennel seed vinaigrette and white port reduction, or butter poached lobster with crispy Kombu noodles and whole roasted shallots, in a lobster sherry fumet. For your main course, you may choose a venison leg filet with venison game sausage and a sauce poivrade, or superb diver sea scallops and shrimp finished with lobster butter and a balsamic reduction. The duck with blood orange sauce is like no other canard à l'orange you ever ate. If you are dissatisfied with your selection, it will be whisked away, no questions asked. Sylvia Moubayed wants to leave her diners delighted and restored, and she strives to make the world a better place through her fine fare and ambience; surely, she has achieved that many meals over.

A terrific cocktail list, and a well chosen selection of wines by the glass and bottle complement your meal. Cav serves a casual affordable lunch with the same high standards in food. In the summer al fresco dining is available on the interior patio. Cav is cozy and accessible but works as well for a special evening. Entrees are in the $23 to $30 range. Reservations are available. Almost everything – the table covers, the chairs, the art - is for sale.

20. Chapinlandia

319 Pocasset Avenue (Olneyville)
Providence, RI 02909
401-464-9499
Lunch, Dinner
$

Many dishes can satisfy cravings you didn't even know you had -- until you taste a particular offering for the first time. Recently, thanks to a hot tip from a guy delivering linens to a Silver Lake restaurant, we found ourselves at Chapinlandia, in a little mini-strip of Guatemalan stores and restaurants on Pocasset Avenue. And it was there that we discovered sopa de patos ("Cow feet soup" in the menu translation).

But we'll get back to that. If you're not familiar with Guatemalan cuisine, we'd heartily recommend a trip to Chapinlandia. It's a clean-looking place with plenty of booths, a well-stocked bar, and, in an adjoining room, a pool table. There's a lot of formica going on, but the tidy look of the place is somehow confidence-inspiring. Not all the servers speak much (if any) English, and while the menu does have translations of the Spanish listings, these are not always helpful. Tamalito de Chipalin, for instance, is "Corn lump w/chipalin." In general, the offerings sound Mexican, but with a difference. No mole, no chimichangas, no enchiladas. No guacamole!

But the pollo a la parilla ($7) – grilled chicken with two tortillas and a salad – is terrific and tasty. The chicken is tender, and the tortillas are soft and flavorful, the flavors vibrant and new but not fiery. Soft tacos with chicken, beef or pork ($3.00) encourage you to eat nothing else, all day. But if you also ordered, in the spirit of adventure, the sopa de patas ($9), you'll be as happy as food can make you (in our case, that's an almost transcendental state). The soup arrives on an oval plate, in a large bowl. Alongside are a couple of lime wedges and a mound of rice. You squeeze the limes into the soup, and you can dump your rice in there too. The soup is dark and aromatic – it smells of beef and cilantro and warm peppers. In it you can see the submerged white pieces that must be the feet of the cow. Taste the soup. It is rich and warming, with intense but not uncomfortable seasoning and a pleasantly unctuous texture probably from the gelatin in the aforementioned hooves. Now that you're wallowing happily in the broth, it's time to eat the feet. The texture is soft, the flavor very mild and not at all organy. Some of the bigger pieces may put you off, and that's OK. The whole experience is rich and satisfying.

Chapinlandia's menu offers many other appealing choices, including a full breakfast lineup. We can't wait to try their huevos rancheros.

21. Chez Pascal

960 Hope Street (Hope Street)
Providence RI 02906
401-421-4422
www.chez-pascal.com
Dinner Tuesday – Saturday
Reservations
$$$

This restaurant underwent a transformation when Kristen and Matt Gennuso took it over a few years ago. They concentrated on classic French bistro cooking and quickly became the darlings of the East Side. The place is romantic and charming and seems to be packed even on weeknights, because the owners have taken great care with every detail. It is also noteworthy that many Providence chefs love this place. We love the food. The chef is on the mark with his soups and salads, and for entrees, the duck is always worth ordering if you aren't tempted by the nightly specials.

Chez Pascal is of the slow food movement, using only seasonal local materials. On a cold winter night, the menu offers cassoulet and a warm cabbage salad with blue cheese and walnuts. In the spring, you will find a grilled steak with trumpet mushrooms or a delicate scallop dish. Chef Matt makes all his own sausage and prosciutto, as well as stocks and meat glazes. With the tremendous attention he pays to all his ingredients, the chef offers consistently first rate dishes, which has earned him a loyal following. He is so interested in sausages that in the summer months on the bucolic lawn across the street, he even operates a gourmet hotdog cart and serves the best hotdog you'll ever taste.

Chez Pascal offers a bistro menu on the weeknights with three courses for $28 per person, exclusive of drinks and tip. It is almost always a very tempting offering and never seems like a sparer version of the regular menu.

22. Chilangos Taqueria and Tequila Bar

447 Manton Avenue (Olneyville)
Providence, RI 02909
401-383-4877
Breakfast, Lunch daily except Wednesday
Dinner except Wednesday, closes early Tuesday evenings
$

When the Brown *Daily Herald* named Chilangos the best Mexican restaurant in Providence, we beat a hasty path to the door. We found it right at the bottom of Atwells Avenue where it bumps into Manton Avenue, a spot known to locals as The Junction. We agree with the Brown students' assessment. Since discovering it for ourselves a year back, we have definitely become regulars. The food is good and fresh and prepared with a light touch. There is none of the heavy cheese sauce; rather, chopped fresh herbs, a drizzle of sour cream, and a sprinkling of queso fresco complement the dishes. The Tostada Tinga, a big favorite, is a crisp corn tortilla covered with shredded chicken in a garlic tomato sauce. We have ventured from head to toe with the beef tongue and the pickled cow's feet. The tacos are fresh soft corn tortillas and offered in many versions such as lean steak, chourico, and chicken. A full range of Mexican goodies is available including burritos, huaraches, quesadillas, pambozas, gorditos, and possibly the best enchiladas we have ever had. The enchiladas verdes, with zingy hot tomatillo sauce and a bouquet of cilantro, tastes so clean and moist and complex that it is hard to believe it is a simple dish.

Chilangos is a charming little spot in the middle of Olneyville, with carved wooden benches and saddles as bar stools. The clientele is largely Hispanic suggesting that the food is authentic. The service is impeccable, and the prices are dirt cheap. The Tinga Tostada and the Taco are less than five dollars together. On the Tequila side of this tacqueria is a serious bar offering many Tequilas and Margarita by the glass is $6.50. A pitcher of Margaritas big enough for six drinks costs $28.00. No wonder Chilangos is busy, and we're always glad it is because we want it to succeed and stay there. Although they do not take reservations and it's packed on weekend nights, just drop in and sip a Margarita as you wait.

23. Chinese Laundry

121 N. Main Street (College Hill)
Providence RI 02906
401-272-8676
www.chineselaundryri.com
Dinner Tuesday –Saturday
$$$$

The Chinese Laundry is a jewel box on North Main Street. Sandwiched between XO and Mill's Tavern, the Laundry offers an entirely different eating experience. In a narrow three story building, the innovative designers have managed to create a second floor lounge and a tiny dining room on the ground level with a glass floor that looks down onto a third space which is a private dining room. There is a bar on each of the floors, and seating for about 44 patrons in the dining areas. The striking décor is all black and red lacquer with subtle painting of bamboo trees, handsome tile flooring and exquisite bathrooms.

Like any jewel box, the contents are precious. Executive Chef Nick Rabar is using the most expensive ingredients like Kobe beef and foie gras, caviar and toro grade tuna. He describes his menu as "traditional Chinese and Japanese food with a contemporary twist." Expect the prices to be precious as well - from $8 to $20 for appetizers, $20 to $45 for entrees. The choices are exciting, from a black truffle sushi to a wok-fried lobster. There is a crab pad thai, kobe lo mein and duck with ramen noodles. Each dish is served at the moment of readiness, lending the opportunity to share the dishes as they reach the table. The table space is so small that serving several dishes at once will be uncomfortable.

Also like any ideal jewel box, it is hard to gain entry. There are no reservations taken for the main dining room. You can while away your time waiting for a table in the upstairs lounge. Indeed, the only guaranteed access to this tiny place is through reserving the private dining room. That room, which seats 10, offers tasting menus only, ranging from eight to ten to twelve courses, with a price tag of $65 for the eight courses and $115 for the twelve. The liquor selections include ten wines by the glass and over a hundred bottles as well as ten choices of sake.

Chinese Laundry was designed with all this in mind: make it special, make it exclusive, and make it worth the wait. The restaurant has the ambience, the chef has the chops, the owners (Chow Fun of Citron, 10 and XO fame) have the **33** pedigree, and the restaurant is unlike any other in town. Definitely give this a go if you can get in.

After we go to press, the Chow Fun Group will open Rick's Roadhouse in late spring of 2008. They describe the décor as down and dirty, with neon signs, pinball machines, whiskey barrels and a "Whiskey Bar". Rick's will serve barbecue, burgers and steaks, along with plenty of fried appetizers. Given the talent of the owners, we assume Rick's will be a high-profile option for lunch on weekdays or dinner seven nights a week.

24. Citron

5 Memorial Boulevard (Downcity)
Providence RI 02903
401-621-9443
www.citronri.com
Lunch weekdays
Dinner nightly
Sunday Brunch
Reservations
$$$

Citron is an attractive downtown restaurant with a creative menu and a wide price range. In the summer, the cheerful yellow umbrellas shade about five of the eight outdoor tables, and in the winter, a very chic décor provides a sophisticated feel to the inside dining area. The restaurant has John Elkhay's stamp all over it – which means it makes a statement. Elkhay knows food, was a top chef when he was cooking, and he has a distinctly creative edge. He has opened at least a half dozen successful restaurants over the past twenty-five years, most recently with the Chow Fun Group.

Citron is designed for all comers: the secretary who might want a pulled pork quesadilla ($8.95) and a Coke for lunch, or her boss, who wants a filet mignon ($24.95) and a $200 bottle of wine. The menu is fun, with offerings like a pappardelle Bolognese, ($17.95) which in this case is made with wild boar sausage and topped with "a sprinkling of expensive parmesan cheese." At lunch, you'll find interesting choices like grilled Hunan chicken salad and a fried eggplant sandwich with goat cheese and roasted tomato aioli. Some of the more interesting dinner items are appetizers such as an ahi tuna tasting which includes spring roll, ceviche, and sesame seared tuna with ginger, wasabi and ponzu, or a duck confit served with frisée, lardoons and garlic chips. The list of entrees begins with "Today's Experimental Dish," which on a warm spring night was lamb sirloin with parsnip purée, baby spinach, and a red currant port reduction. Wines by the glass start at a reasonable $6.50 and head upwards for the cognoscenti.

Desserts would satisfy any reasonable craving with choices like hot molten lava cake, coconut crème brulée and carpaccio of fresh fruit with pineapple sorbet. Dessert prices are in the six dollar range.

A couple of problems: Citron does not have an efficient outdoor seating plan. We arrived when two precious empty tables were available and no takers were in sight. Not allowed to seat ourselves, we were sent indoors to the hostess. By the time we emerged, those seats were taken by later arrivals, who could not be asked to leave. Also, for some reason only some of the tables have umbrellas, which means hats and sunglasses for comfortable seating.

Citron is one of four (Capitol Grille, Rira, Union Station Brewery) restaurants behind the old Providence train station. Its proximity to Waterplace Park makes it a great spot for WaterFire and an easy lunch or dinner restaurant for downcity dwellers. Those of us who drive there face an added charge for parking, which with a stamp from the restaurant is six dollars.

25. Costantino's Ristorante & Caffe

265 Atwells Avenue (Federal Hill)
Providence, RI 02903
401-528-1100
Dinner nightly
Reservations
$$$-$$$$

Right across from Venda Ravioli on DePasquale Plaza, Costantino's offers some of the very best Italian fare in Providence. Unlike its informal sibling on the plaza, Costantino's Ristorante is a "let's go out for a Big Deal dinner" kind of place, and it will not disappoint.

When you enter from the plaza, you're in a lounge. There are a few people enjoying a Bellini or a cocktail here, but it's not just a staging area for impatient people who don't have their table yet. It's a real venue on its own, with comfortable seating and views out to the Plaza. Up the staircase is the dining room, quite fancy with tables spaced at intervals that actually permit you to have – and hear – a private conversation. The menu is extensive and appetizing, the service professional, warm, but never intrusive.

If they're in season, soft-shell crabs, sautéed and served on a bed of wilted arugula ($11.95) will beckon you. The bitterness of the arugula is a nice foil against the sweetness of the crabmeat. It's a delicious, elegant dish. Pastas, as you might expect from a member of the Venda Ravioli family, are a sure thing, although we're especially addicted to the pappardelle con porcini e prosciutto ($13.95), wide pasta ribbons with sautéed wild mushrooms and ham, topped with pecorino romano. Fabulous!

Now we're getting into territory that really takes planning, unless you're a Sumo wrestler in training. If you have, say, the softshells, and follow them with a nice pasta, will you have room for the bistecca alla fiorentina ($29.95)? It's a 14-ounce T-Bone drizzled with extra virgin olive oil (and some lemon juice, if you wish. You should wish). It is as close as we've come here to replicating bistecca alla fiorentina we've had in Tuscany. Veal chops, lamb, chicken, fish, are all well-prepared and beautifully presented, but oh, that T-bone.

Desserts are good, too, but pastas and entrees (primi e secondi, to be precise) are really the main event at Costantino's.

Costantino's has about 20 wines available by the glass and 300 choices on its fairly priced wine list You can find a Ruffino Ducale Gold Chianti Classico for about $45 and a 1998 Antinori Solaia for around $225, with plenty of choices in between.

There are so many great Italian restaurants in Providence, it's hard to decide on a favorite. Costantino's will always be close to the top of our list. Free valet parking is available, a major plus on Atwells Avenue, especially on a Friday or Saturday night. Reservations are advisable.

26. Cuban Revolution

50 Aborn Street (Downcity)
60 Valley Street (Olneyville)
Providence, RI
401-331-8829 (Downcity)
401-632-0649 (Olneyville)
www.thecubanrevolution.com
Lunch, Dinner daily
Reservations
$

In 2007, Cuban Revolution moved to splendid new digs. The hot little sandwich shop which created a cult following in its tiny space on Washington Street is now handsomely housed in a space around the corner on 50 Aborn Street. Cuban Revolution can host 65 diners and offer them Cuba Libres along with their food. Owners Ed and Mary Morabito now added a second Cuban Revolution in a larger and fabulous space on Valley Street. Cuban Revolution prides itself on food, décor and music, all reflecting Morabito's politically active mind. Ed Morabito hails from the sixties counterculture, when "challenging the norm was the norm." That paean to individual expression is evident in the Che Guevara berets worn by the waitstaff and the oversized paintings created by Angel Quinones.

Cuban Revolution is busy at lunch when the downcity eatery offers, at just $3 - $4, exotic food like tostones, crunchy fried plantains with an adobo sauce, or croquetas de jamo. The higher priced items include the modestly named "World's Best Steak," for $6.58, or the "World's Best Pork," for the same price. If your cholesterol count is too low, you can give it a nice bump with "World's Best Cuban Sandwich" (at $6.58 – that number must mean something) – roast pork, ham, salami, swill cheese, mayo, mustard, grilled and pressed so everything smooshes together in a revolutionary way.

In the evening, Cuban revolution swings with live music, a full bar and main course entrees that cost downward of $11.50. The space is hip and edgy, with an inexpensive menu and a friendly and warm atmosphere.

27. Don Shula's 347 Grille

21 Atwells Avenue (Federal Hill)
Providence RI 029003
401-709-0347
Breakfast, Lunch, Dinner daily
Reservations

Don Shula's has it just right for a restaurant next to a sports center: it's in the Hilton, a jump shot away from the Dunk. Shula's, which is named for the famous Hall of Fame, Super Bowl winning, first undefeated season NFL football coach, has more than 26 restaurants around the United States and Providence has landed Don Shula's XXVII. (Kind of hard to imagine a restaurant called "Bill Belichick's," isn't it?) The restaurant has a handsome interior, big booths, pigskin walls, flat-screen televisions all over, and a manly menu that will easily please the men's ladies. It's the kind of place where one would feel equally comfortable dressed up or dressed down.

Don Shula's serves big beefy steaks cut from Coach Shula's own Angus cattle, which he raises on ranches he co-owns. The Shula Steaks are Certified Angus Beef, custom cut and "our aging process make up the award winning SHULA CUTS, which are better than Prime." We rate steaks with our taste buds and we'd have to say that the beef here is first-rate. Best ever? That's a stretch, but certainly top-notch. The prices are in the $30 range for a big sirloin, cooked at 500 degrees and seasoned with the Shula special spices. The menu offers plenty of other choices like terrific fresh salads, sandwiches and seafood. The place is packed on sports nights, but is a lovely option for a quiet (and surprisingly reasonable) lunch. The service is present when you need it, not when you don't.

28. DownCity

50 Weybosset Street (Downcity)
Providence RI 02903
401-331-9217
www.downcityfood.com
Lunch, Dinner daily
Brunch on weekends
Reservations
$$-$$$

DownCity has earned "institution" status. It has been a beloved part of the Providence dining scene for about 15 years. This doesn't make it an old fogey; in fact, it is brand new. A 2006 fire destroyed the old DownCity Diner, and a stunning new restaurant with a shortened name has taken its place. The bigger and warmer new digs invite you to relax and dine. The main floor has 100 seats, and with its handsome bar and giant flat screen television, many folks enjoy lingering. An upstairs mezzanine has 50 additional seats. The sophisticated space has the signature warm DownCity orange with cream colored leather banquettes.

The DownCity food concept remains the same: an American bistro with moderately priced good food and great cocktails. There's an emphasis on comfort food with the popular DownCity meatloaf as well as the buffalo chicken salad. Braised steak tacos with soft corn tortillas, shredded cabbage and roasted tomatillo guacamole provide a tempting south of the border touch. Dinner prices run from $9.50 for a burger with boursin cheese, bacon, lettuce, tomatoes, onions and hand cut fries to $23.50 for the New York Sirloin. Other entrees include scallops, crab cakes and shrimp risotto. Wines by the glass run about $7.50.

DownCity is open seven days a week for lunch, dinner, brunch and late night. It's popular with members of the gay and lesbian communities, downtown business folk, college students and East Siders.

29. El Rancho Grande

311 Plainfield Street (Olneyville)
Providence 02909
401-275-0855
www.elranchogrande.com
Breakfast, Lunch, Dinner daily
$-$$

When you walk into El Rancho Grande at lunchtime, you're likely to find a few tables of Spanish-speaking guys watching soccer on the TV over the bar. In front of them are platters of food, which they're eating avidly but without paying much attention, as if they've been eating the same stuff all their lives.

Well, they have. This is the real deal – some of the freshest, most authentic, tastiest Mexican food we've tried in Providence. Maria Meza, the chef, cooks the way mothers cook in Mexico – if they're really, really good cooks. The place is right across from the off-ramp from Route 6, so it's easy to miss if you just whiz by, but if you do, hook a U. Not only is the food good, but the welcome is warm. The space is warm as well, painted a soft yellow. It is immaculate, comfortable and fresh, with 44 seats and a bar serving wine and beer.

El Rancho Grande features a few items not necessarily found on Mexican menus elsewhere in town. Menudo, for example, the tripe soup with peppers and chick peas is rich and spicy, with that marvelous slippery texture that comes from long slow cooking with animal innards. A bowl is $7.00, and along with a few tortillas, could be a meal, especially if you start off with the very good guacamole ($3.00). Barbacoa, goat to you, is available in tacos ($1.50 each) or as a house special. The meat is emphatic but not too goaty, with a spicy rub that enhances the goat's flavor. The meat is tender and perfect. Enchiladas verdes ($7.50) are a definite cut above the tired usual type. The sauce is vibrant, and you can taste the ingredients – tomatillos, goat cheese, onions. Salsa is homemade and brings your mouth to life.

Everything we tried at El Rancho Grande tasted as if it had just been made that morning. When Maria came out of the kitchen as we were finishing our meal, she confirmed that in fact it had been made that morning.

In addition to the beer and wines, there are fruit juices and Mexican sodas. A bottle or two of Negra Modelo is ideal, but even Diet Coke tastes like the elixir of the gods with this food. Go on a field trip and find out what light, fresh, authentic Mexican food really tastes like.

30. Fleming's

1 West Exchange Street (Downcity)
Providence RI 02903
401-533-9000
www.flemingssteakhouse.com
Dinner Nightly
Reservations
$$$ - $$$$

Fleming's accompanies its sumptuous surroundings with its sensational steaks. The place is gorgeous, with cherry-paneled walls and large overhead lighting fixtures with opaque shades that cast a warm red hue. The booths are red leather which adds to the warmth and a handsome bar lines the back of the dining room. Fleming's has gotten it just right all the way around. The service is excellent, the food equally impressive, and the wine list is exceptional with 100 wines available by both glass and bottle. No doubt about it, dinner at Fleming's feels very special.

It's not cheap, but the steaks are USDA Prime and a 16-ounce strip steak runs $35.95, which is about ten dollars less than some of the other local steak houses. There are ribeyes, and porterhouses, filets and strips, along with veal chops and lamb chops, chicken and prime rib. We sampled three different steaks on our visit, each of which was cooked to perfection. Three sauces are available, béarnaise, peppercorn and Madeira. Each was very good. The wedge salad was cool and crisp with a rich bacony blue cheese dressing. Sides like shoestring potatoes and creamed spinach were perfect, and others like creamed corn gratinée with gruyere and parmesan, or chipotle cheddar mac and cheese looked very tempting. On the seafood side, the menu offers a tuna mignon with poppy seed au poivre, Alaskan King Crab legs and Maine lobster with drawn butter, all superb.

The wine list is not only expansive, it is arranged in a very accessible way. Each category of wine is listed by intensity of grape, so the diner who wants a fuller glass of wine can choose with confidence. Interestingly enough, there is a range of prices among the more intense wines, so that one glass might cost $8.50, while another might be $20, but it is possible to get a very good glass at the lower price point.

We ordered a dessert sampler which gave us a small serving of each item on the dessert menu. Baked peach cobbler was as good as the chocolate lava cake, and the crème brulée rivaled the cheesecake with blueberry sauce. We treated ourselves very well at Fleming's, but the place makes you feel so good, you can't help yourself.

31. Garden Grille Café

727 East Avenue (Hope Street)
Pawtucket RI 02860
401-726-2826
www.gardengrillecafe.com
Lunch, Dinner daily
Brunch on Sunday
Reservations for 6 or more
$$

Technically, this dining spot is in Pawtucket, but if you walk south across the parking lot and then one short block, you are right on the East Side. We had to include it because it is not only Providence's only wood-fired vegetarian restaurant, but it is consistently good, and it obviously meets a need. For eleven years, the Garden Grille has offered selections which are in short supply but in long demand, as evidenced by the lines of patrons waiting to be seated.

Over the years, owner Rob Yaffe has honed his menu and has added great charm and warmth to his interior. The café seats about 50 people in a warm toned dining room with booths and tables. Fresh organic juices can accompany menu items that include, for example, a wood-grilled pear and asparagus salad, and Cajun spice encrusted tempeh. There is a variety of quesadillas and pizzas, and you can select a salad from the many delicious options. Liquor, including organic vodkas and cocktails with fresh squeezed fruit juices, is available. The prices are moderate for all the offerings.

32. Geppetto's Pizzeria

57 DePasquale Plaza (Federal Hill)
Providence, RI 02903
401-270-3003
www.geppettospizzeria.com
Lunch, Dinner daily
$ - $$

Few things in Providence – heck, few things in life – are as pleasant as lunch on the terrace at Geppetto's on a nice day. The people-watching is terrific, the pizza is delicious, and if you have a newspaper or magazine to read and a glass of Geppetto's very nice, very reasonably-priced ($5.95) house Chianti with your meal, you experience a powerful sensation of well-being.

Geppetto's Grilled Pizzeria (of course it's the pizza that's grilled, not the restaurant) features a signature thin-crust pie in two sizes: "Personal 10-inch" or "Large 14-inch." The Personal pie is perfect for one person, as you might expect. The toppings range from classic cheese and tomato ($6.95 for Personal) to more creative options like the "California Club" ($10.95) with grilled chicken, avocado, bacon, mozzarella, tomatoes, lettuce and mayo. OK, you try it. Probably fabulous.

The grilled crusts are wonderful – almost paper-thin, with nicely charred edges and just enough heft to support the toppings. They come sliced into bite-sized squares, not wedges, which makes eating them a far more dignified procedure. They also offer a traditional oven pizza in one (16-inch) size that'll feed three or four. Good, but not so good as the grilled model.

If you order the fried calamari appetizer, you'll get a BIG plate of perfectly-fried golden rings tossed with hot cherry peppers and a little bowl of hot red sauce for dipping. There is plenty of squid for two on the plate.

Geppetto's has a tiny wine list, but on it we noticed a 2001 Antinori Chianti Classico "Peppole" for $39. That is a serious bargain for a top-notch Chianti from the best year ever, maybe, in Chianti. Go ahead and order that California Club 'za and make your day with a great deal on a great wine. Act now – it has to be going fast.

33. Gracie's

194 Washington Street (Downcity)
Providence, RI 02903
401-272-7811
www.graciesprov.com
Dinner Tuesday-Sunday
Reservations
$$$ - $$$$

Among the stars in Rhode Island's restaurant sky, few if any shine as brightly as Gracie's. Chef Joseph Hafner's talent, creativity and dedication to the freshest ingredients result in a menu that will drive you insane with indecision and then make you blissfully content with whatever you finally choose.

When you enter Gracie's, a host or hostess immediately greets you warmly. By the time you reach your table, you're already settling into the restaurant's benign and reassuring embrace. Gracie's signature stars twinkle hospitably. Soft lighting achieves the nearly impossible feat of being low enough to be flattering and bright enough to read menus. But if you need more light, your server has a flashlight ready for you. Because the tables are spaced at civilized intervals, your group can get merry without wrecking someone else's evening.

The menu offers a seven-course tasting alternative as well as a la carte selections. If you're trying to get to Trinity Rep, there's a pre-theater menu with three courses that would probably be the smart way to go. But for us, a hasty dinner at Gracie's would just be a crime, because you really want to settle back and let the kitchen and your servers take care of you for a couple of hours.

The menu changes seasonally, which means that many of the courses we enjoyed on a winter evening won't be available if you visit in May or September. You may, however, be lucky enough to see the tuna crudo ($18), a dish so gorgeous to look at you almost hate to eat it. But you do, and find that it's on a higher but parallel plane as that occupied by tuna tartare. Oblong pieces of sushi-grade tuna are arranged on a long narrow white plate and garnished with olive oil, cucumber, Easter egg radish, kumquat confit and creme fraiche. The textures and flavors keep their identities but combine to make each mouthful a slightly different experience from the one before. The kitchen makes exceptional gnocchi; the wintertime rendition ($12) is made with braised oxtail, black trumpet mushrooms, celery root puree and fontina. The little individual gnocchi are featherlike yet soak up the flavors they accompany perfectly. Two wonderful soups, one composed of celeriac with trout fritters, and one of butternut squash with tiny caramelized bits of apples were both remarkable.

Among the main courses, venison loin with venison sausage, roasted fennel, sweet potato bread and juniper venison jus ($34.00) was outstanding, the meat tender and rich-tasting, not gamy or dry as venison so often can be. The Maple Leaf Farms duck, with chestnut bread pudding, charred brussels sprouts and green apple with blood orange glaze ($28) arrived medium-rare, as requested. The skin was crisp and the ducky layer of fat just underneath seemed to tenderize the meat as you ate it. Rich duck tastes and melting textures made this one of the best duck entrees we've encountered, and not just in Providence: anywhere. The "bread pudding" is really a scrumptious old-fashioned stuffing like the one your Grandma with the Afghan used to make, but much, much better.

A strip steak from Wolfe's Neck Farm ($35) and grouper ($27), subbing for a listed Maryland striped bass that Chef Hafner cut from the menu, were both exceptional. Flavors throughout are bright and focused, presentation appealing and artistic. At our table, every plate was clean at the end of the main course.

Gracie's wine list is not mammoth, but the well chosen selections reflect the restaurant's preference for small producers, of wines as well as foods. Bottles range from about $34 and up.

Desserts are a bit of an anticlimax, but anything might be. They are creative and seem to emphasize chocolate, not at all a bad thing. It is worth noting that a chocolate tartlet made with dark chocolate and fleur du sel provided a major thrill and was trumpeted as completely original and satisfying. There is also an artisanal cheese plate from Farmstead Cheese that is worth exploring if you're still feeling adventuresome. Or hungry.

An evening at Gracie's is not inexpensive, but there is no reason to expect it to be. It's a serious restaurant that could compete and thrive in any market, with intelligent and thoughtful service and food that is just plain wonderful. It is in no way pretentious, but it lets you know that it means business, and the prices reflect the care that goes into both acquisition and preparation. Special occasion? Go to Gracie's. They won't let you down.

34. Guido's

100 Hope Street (Fox Point)
Providence RI 02906
401-273-0812
http://guidosri.tripod.com
Dinner Wednesday - Sunday
Reservations
No credit cards, BYOB
$$

On a 6 degree winter night, we were happily ensconced in a tiny East Side hideaway, when a lovely woman walked in with her bottle of wine. She happened to know someone in our party and told us she was there without her husband because he was working and it was her favorite place. It is a comment on the tone of Guido's that it was comfortable enough for her to walk in, and a further comment came from her, saying she wanted nothing more than their eggplant and pasta, knowing it would be satisfying, as always. Guido's is that kind of place – safe, welcoming, beyond cozy. The food is straightforward Italian, pastas and sausage, veal piccata and calamari -- nothing fancy, just consistently flavorful and satisfying.

The prices are moderate; you can bring your own wine, but you can't use a credit card. You can make a reservation if the phone isn't off the hook. Some nights the lines are out the door, and other nights you are one of two tables. But we're glad it is still there after twenty years, at the corner of Hope and John. We're thrilled that we can stop by for some delicious garlic bread, a good salad, some perfect calamari, a lightly spiced sausage and pasta or an order or eggplant rollatini, and walk out paying no more than $60 for two, including a $4 per bottle corkage fee.

Don't go if you are looking for 4-star Italian dining, but do go if you want a fine meal, an embracing ambience, good service and low prices.

35. Haruki East

172 Wayland Avenue (Wayland Square)
Providence, RI 02906
401-223-0332
www.harukisushi.com
Lunch Monday-Saturday
Dinner - nightly
Reservations on weeknights, weekends for 6 or more
$$$

Wrapped around a corner in Wayland Square, Haruki East is about the fanciest sushi place in Providence, but it doesn't look it from the street. The windows are screened by a blue gray scrim giving the place a "we're closed" look which we find a bit standoffish. But evidently we're the only ones, because Haruki East operates at capacity most of the time, and at peak meal hours you may have to wait for a table, or even a seat at the curved sushi counter.

Once inside and seated, you'll find that Haruki East is visually inviting. Pale wood and sea-blue walls create a crisp clean look that's not so austere as many of the sushi spots in town. You know you're at the high end of the sushi spectrum, and a glance at the extensive menu will confirm that. Haruki East is not a cheap eat. It's a popular spot for couples and probably qualifies as a bit of a splurge for the Brown and RISD students who stab their chopsticks into each other's California rolls and sip sakes from Haruki's extensive list.

Sushi is, of course, the feature, and it is fresh, carefully prepared and presented, although to our minds the portions tend to be a bit large. If you believe that sushi is meant to be eaten in one bite, as we do, you'll have to compromise your principles here as many of the raw-fish items on offer are just too big for that. Then what? Do you try to saw your sushi in half with your chopsticks? Tough to do, especially with a resilient slice of octopus or giant clam sitting on top of the rice. Put it in your mouth and bite off half? Sloppy, with rice often cascading down your front and the now-naked piece of fish dripping soy sauce and wasabi. Prices of sushi and sashimi items vary according to availability but a sushi-sashimi combination entrée will be about $21.

In addition to its extensive sushi and sashimi options, Haruki East has a full menu of Japanese appetizers and main dishes. Beef teriyaki ($16.50) is always a crowd pleaser, as is tempura ($13.50. If raw fish just doesn't float your boat but you like seafood when it's cooked, salmon teriyaki ($15.50) or shiromi sakana ($14.50), a grilled fish with wasabi cream sauce, should satisfy your palate. At lunchtime we heartily recommend the Katsu Don, a bowl of rice with fried pork, scrambled egg and broth poured on top. It's a Japanese on-the-run staple, and it's delicious, filling and cheap.

Haruki East is part of a family of Japanese restaurants that also includes Haruki Express on Waterman Street near Thayer, which we have not tried.

36. Hemenway's Seafood Grill & Oyster Bar
21 South Main St (College Hill)
Providence, RI 02903
401-351-8570
www.hemenwaysrestaurant.com
Lunch, Dinner daily
Reservations
$$$

Walk into Hemenway's at dinnertime on a Saturday night and you'll swear you're not in Providence anymore. The place has a real big-city vibe, starting with the look of it. Set on the ground floor of an office building overlooking the Providence River, the bright two-story room is all glass walls, tiered seating, a booming bar up front, and that kinetic bustle that says, "This place is cooking."

When you're seated and your server has handed you your menu, you can just relish the selections. Indeed oysters, as well as clams, mussels, and scallops and lobsters - up to five pounds - will surely tempt you. You can choose plain grilled fish from the many offerings and the chef's specialties, more elaborate preparations based on the same fresh seafood. Tucked away in a corner of the menu, you will see meat options for people who came here by mistake, and in another corner are "New England Traditions" – fried fish to you.

Among the appetizers, you can't go wrong with oysters and clams from the raw bar. A Hemenway's feature is Portuguese grilled littlenecks ($8.95), a half-dozen or so juicy, briny clams, just popped open from the heat, in a tomato-based sauce with good-sized chunks of chorizo and a couple of slices of grilled bread to soak up the sauce. You could stop right there and go home happy. New England-style clam chowder ($4) for a cup and $5 for a bowl) is rich but not thick and floury. Lobster bisque may be too rich for some, but it is flavorful with big pieces of lobster, sherry and butter.

Some mains belong in that not-very-exclusive Providence institution, the Too Much On The Plate Club. If you order a grilled fish and a side, you should be very happy. If you order, say, the Shrimp Scampi ($18.95), it may overwhelm you when it arrives because there's just so much in the bowl: cappellini, scampi, roasted tomatoes, garlic, lots of broth, bread. Many of the Chef's Specialties espouse the abbondanza approach and if you've already had a hearty appetizer, plenty of bread and a salad before your main course arrives, you may suffer from buyer's remorse.

Service is friendly and accommodating, but Hemenway's is hopping, and there are occasional glitches. Sometimes salad or appetizers are not bussed before the mains arrive, causing an unseemly shuffle during which you hold your salad plate over your head, while your server or runner slides the entrée in front of you, then takes the salad plate with one hand while delivering the other entrée to your dining partner who also holds his or her salad aloft. Amusing, but also somewhat alarming.

Hemenway's has an extensive, fairly priced and interesting wine list and a good selection of wines by the glass, priced from $5.7 - $10.00. The list features a selection of "seafood reds" which included a number of Shirazes and Petite Syrahs – generally big fruity wines which we would not normally recommend with fish. However, many of Hemenway's menu options feature big flavors – lots of garlic and tomato and spicy chorizos – so if you are a red wine drinker, why not get yourself a bottle of Foppiano Petite Syrah ($39.00) with your Arctic char?

37. India

1070 Hope Street (Hope Street)
Providence RI 02906
401-421-2600
www.indiarestaurant.com
Lunch, Dinner daily

When the weather's good, India is one of the most pleasant places in Providence. The restaurant has a pretty patio, and you can order a perfectly preposterous plate of pepper pappadums for only $2.00 while you consider the rest of your meal options.

Even in the dark and gloom of winter, India is a lovely spot. The dining room, while darkish, is spacious and attractive and feels authentically subcontinental. The food is zesty and appealing, with everything from intriguing dinner salads like warm seafood salad with tiger shrimps and sea scallops sautéed in oil and garlic with baby spinach and garlic naan ($10). The service is friendly and accommodating. India offers a full lineup of vegetarian curries including gobhi aloo, with cauliflower, curried potatoes and tomatoes zipped with cilantro, cumin seeds and turmeric, for $9.00 at dinner.

In general, the dishes at India are seasoned for tame American palates. The "robust curries" are listed in ascending order of hotness, and you can request additional heat in any one of them. So if the vindaloo ($11 with lamb at dinner) doesn't contain enough napalm for you, the restaurant reminds you that you can dial it up.

We especially like the lamb saag, the tender meat cooked to melting softness with spinach and cream. It's rich and satisfying, served with a fragrant ring of basmati rice. Ask your server for the soup of the day; each one is almost always well worth it. We also applaud the biryanis, in which meat or a vegetable is simmered together with basmati and pineapple, raisins, cashews, cilantro and a fabulous and aromatic blend of spices. Prices range from $10 for the vegetable biryani to $15 for the house special, with mushroom, chicken, lamb, shrimp and scallops.

India has wines, beer and lassi, the refreshing yogurt shake, coffee and Darjeeling tea.

8. Julian's

318 Broadway (West End)
Providence RI 02909
401-861-1770
www.juliansprovidence.com
Breakfast, Lunch, Dinner daily
Reservations

If Julian's is real, the people behind it *should* look just like the people who work and dine there: heavily tattooed, youngish raffish and hippish. If it's not real – if the owners are investors who live in Barrington and sail on the weekends – then you really have to hand it to them. Julian's is totally convincing. From décor to menu to staff to patrons, Julian's is a fully realized artsy joint with good food to boot.

The minute you walk in, even when it's crowded, someone greets you in a friendly fashion and either directs you to a table or advises you on waiting time and offers you a drink. If you wait at the bar, look around. If you're over 40, you will feel somewhat Martian. Get over it! Julian's has a nice upbea vibe and if you get a menu to peruse, you be intrigued by th presentation.

"Light Fare" options include house fried tortilla chips wit spiced black bean pumpkin dip ($5.50) and "Blazing Naan chopped budaball ham, pineapple, swiss, baby spinach, swee chile sauce." A small order is $5.00, a large is $10.00. Entrée include a variety of vegetarian and vegan choices, such as th vegan Monte Cristo with tofu turkey and soy cheese for $12.5 and pumpkin gnocchi with mission figs, roasted pepper sliced almonds and arugula for $16.50. But you can also div into a "Hammered Sirloin with Bermuda onion tempur pommes frites and bleu cheese catsup" for $19.50 and ge yourself a nice Saint Francis Red wine for $8.00 a glass.

Salads are especially tasty at Julian's. The brunch offering which are available all day until dinnertime, include a variet of sandwiches. If you're ravenous, try the " Booyah! Burger with candied thick sliced bacon, caramelized apple, dresse arugula and cheddar on a bulky roll.

Our question: with food like this, how do the regulars kee their tattoos from stretching like lava lamp blobs?

39. Kabob and Curry
261 Thayer Street (College Hill)
Providence RI 02906
401-273-8844
www.kabobandcurry.com
Lunch, Dinner daily
Sunday buffet
Reservations
$$

This is a truly pleasant spot for Indian food. The waitstaff is s gracious and polite that the customers feel pampered. Th food is not unlike what one might find at most America Indian restaurants, noticeably, chicken tikka masala and lam roganjosh and myriad biryanis. But its quality is certain superior to most Indian restaurants. The naans and all th sauces, whether masala or curry, are fragrant and seductiv The space is simple and the service is quick, which mear you can have a tasty dinner before scooting across the stre for a film at the Avon, knowing you'll make it on time. Ther is a small but accomplished bar at Kabob and Curry, servin imaginative cocktails. The wine list is affordable and well selected, making it easy to pair wine with Indian food.

Indeed, the owner, Sanjiv Dhar, is such an elegant and gracious presence that the ambience is no surprise. Kabob and Curry has graced Thayer Street for more than a dozen years, watching many other places come and go. We imagine it will be there as long as Mr. Dhar wishes it to be part of the Thayer Street scene.

40. Kartabar

284 Thayer Street (College Hill)
Providence RI 02906
401-331 8111
www.kartabar.com
Lunch, Dinner daily
Reservations
$$

Kartabar has been packing folks into its dark, sexy space for the last six years. The reason is the very good well-priced food and the always attentive service. Kartabar comes into its own late at night when it attracts a young crowd of Euro nightclubbers, but it is also busy at lunchtime when it bustles with college students stopping in for a great pizza or top notch soup. Starting with a hot cheesy onion soup, a creamy tomato basil soup and a crispy pizza with caramelized onions, tomatoes, spinach and cheese, a recent lunch added up to $22 for two, which included beverage as well.

At dinner, the options step up a bit with options like a filet mignon with gorgonzola and red wine demi-glace for $20, or Tuscany scallops with roasted garlic and tomatoes in a white wine Dijon sauce for $19. Kartabar is in an enviable spot with the Thayer Street crowds ever available. Owner Philippe Maatouk keeps a close eye on his operation and makes sure the place remains attractive to his clientele. He describes his food as Mediterranean and his atmosphere as casual, and we agree. An extensive cocktail list and great selections of wine by the glass for about $6.50 complement the food.

We also appreciate the breezy open French doors in the summer, which almost always frame diners having lunch or a cocktail. Finally, if you can't make it to Kartabar in Providence, you can always hit the Mexican branch in Quintana Roo. Check out their website for all the details.

41. Kurrents

525 S. Water Street (Fox Point)
Providence RI 02903
401-437-6777
www.kurrentsrestaurant.com
Lunch, Dinner daily
Reservations
$$

Kurrents sits on the Providence River just inside the Hurricane Barrier, and offers good waterside dining with food and spirits sure to satisfy arriving yachtsmen and folks who want a meal with a view. It's a contemporary and attractive space that once housed Grappa and, more recently, Moda, both of which sadly closed after unsuccessful runs. We hope that Theo Spiritus has the winning formula to keep this spot in business. Spiritus managed the popular Thayer Street restaurant, Paragon, for years and he has brought similarly priced fare to Kurrents, with prime beef burgers served on Ciabatta bread with lettuce, tomato and fries for about $8.00. The pizza menu offers five options from the classic tomato, mozzarella and basil, to buffalo pizza, with chicken and cheddar. Their grilled pizzas have thin crusts and serve at least four generously. Other dishes include pastas, fish and steaks, priced between $15 and $20, including sides. There is a sandwich menu, five or six salad entrées and an interesting set of appetizers that work as bar food. Wines by the glass are priced between $5.50 and $7, which we think is a reasonable by city standards.

Some of the sauces could be tweaked and improved, and the salad dressings could have more flavor and subtlety, but all the ingredients are fresh and first rate. Still, it's the location that puts Kurrents on the map.

42. La Hacienda

1955 Westminster Street (Olneyville)
Providence RI 02909
401-273-5384
Breakfast, Lunch, Dinner daily
$-$$

In the heart of Olneyville Square, this immaculate restaurant offers authentic Mexican food. La Hacienda is cheerfully painted in hues of siena and lime green, with many posters and photographs of Mexico lining the pretty walls. Our waitress even wore an embroidered Mexican blouse, and it is easy to see the great effort put into the restaurant. It is a sister restaurant to La Hacienda at 603 Plainfield Pike, which is really more of a diner, with an equally pleasant wait staff and good food. La Hacienda is open for all three meals, serving authentic dishes like pupusas (pork and cheese filled bread), tostadas, tacos, pozole, poles, and chile relleno. La Hacienda has a beer and wine license, which is a plus. It is clear that Mexican food is finally making successful inroads into Rhode Island, and La Hacienda's owners, Ricardo and Camlin Rivera, offer a bright clean space in which to enjoy it. The restaurant has booths for four, tables for two and seats about 40 people.

The guacamole, which is a real marker for good Mexican food, was fresh and appetizing, although we happily added our hot salsa to the mix. The pupusas are just right when it's cold and you're hungry. For $1.50 each, you should definitely give them a try. The house specialties include tampiqueno, a grilled sirloin with cheese, onion, enchilada, rice, beans, guacamole and tortilla salad ($10.95.) Chicken a la plancha (grilled chicken) comes with fries or plantains for $8.

43. La Laiterie at Farmstead

188 Wayland Avenue (Wayland Square)
Providence, RI 02906
401-274-7177
www.farmsteadinc.com
Dinner Tuesday -Saturday
Reservations for 6 or more
$$$

In a perfect world, every neighborhood would have a great little restaurant within walking distance of its homes. The place would be cozy, attractive, friendly, not insanely expensive – and the food would be terrific and consistent. What? You say there's a place like that in your neighborhood? Then you must near live Wayland Square. Because that's where La Laiterie is.

Farmstead, the stellar cheesemonger's shop on Wayland Avenue, complemented its venue a few years ago with an adjunct wine bar and bistro that has become one of the very best places to eat in Providence. La Laiterie's food – and its wine selections – would make it a destination anywhere. But it also has an authentic neighborhood feel and unpretentiousness that makes you want to return again and again.

The entrance is almost uninviting – just a door next to the door of the cheese store. But once inside, you find that the space is bigger than it looks from the outside – narrow, but deep, and done in warm tones that are welcoming and somehow suggest that the food will be appealing, too. La Laiterie doesn't take reservations for parties fewer than six (our only peeve, but a peeve nonetheless) so you may wind up waiting at the bar for a table. Worse things could happen, since the wines by the glass are interesting and delicious. As an aperitif, you might try the Burgans Albarino ($8), a razor-sharp, dry Spanish white. (If they still have it – wine selections change frequently.)

The menu varies with the seasons and emphasizes local and organic foods like sweet, succulent Bomster scallops from Stonington and beef from Vermont: we suggest you order the flatiron steak ($6) if it's on the menu. In season, produce comes directly from local farmers' markets. And, of course, there's an irresistible array of cheese choices. The cooking is flavorful, creative and distinctive, with fresh turns on old favorites that give them new life. Even the chicken livers we tried one evening ($11) were exceptional – rare inside, almost-crunchy outside, and frankly delicious.

Under no circumstances go without a serving of biscuits ($6). Ethereally fluffy and flecked with chives, they put you in a good mood immediately. And it's a mood you'll stay in until you have to leave.

44. L'Antica Trattoria at St. Bart's Club
66 Sophia Street (Olneyville)
Providence, RI 02909
401-942-0640
Lunch Friday, Saturday
Dinner Tuesday- Sunday
Reservations for 6 or more
$$

Sometimes we stumble across a place we never knew was there, and it is our good fortune. Such was the case with L'Antica Trattoria at St. Bart's Club in Silver Lake, which has been serving good Southern Italian fare for over thirty years. We acknowledge our ignorance in not knowing about it before, but now that we do, we will return.

The restaurant is on a quiet street off Pocasset Avenue, but on a Friday night, there is a stream of cars all heading for the spacious spot, and two big parking lots are full. From the moment we saw the Trattoria, we had a pleasant surprise. A newly renovated exterior stands out in the neighborhood, and inside, there is a warm, spacious dining room. Immediately on being seated we were brought a basket of crusty, tasty Italian bread and handed menus that offered much of the fare we would find on Federal Hill at a fraction of the cost. For example, spaghetti with clams in a marinara sauce was $8.95 and a 14-ounce sirloin was $14.95.

We have since learned that the calamari at L'Antica Trattoria at St. Bart's Club is considered the best in the state by a large cadre of fans. Rino's antipasto included speck, a dried beef sliced paper thin, in a light dressing that complemented the meat. Mozzarella, sausage, calamari, radishes and peppers rounded out the platter. A seafood antipasto includes smelts that were so popular they went as fast as French fries. An appetizer of bruschetta with white beans on toasted garlic bread was totally pleasing at $4.95. and the entrée of housemade sausage and sautéed mushrooms in marinara sauce came with spaghetti for $13.95.

Trattoria at St. Bart's Club has attentive, professional service, a completely convivial atmosphere and a straightforward menu that has been prepared lovingly by the owners who live next door. It is definitely worth a visit.

45. L'Epicureo

311 Westminster Street (Downcity)
Providence RI 02903
401-861-8990
www.lepicureo.com
Dinner Tuesday - Saturday
Reservations
$$$ - $$$$

L'Epicureo is a grand restaurant in the Hotel Providence. It is dramatically appointed with floor to ceiling faux Da Vinci and Botticelli paintings and elaborate chandeliers. Its approach is formal, and its ambience and prices definitely shout "special occasion!" It is, and has been, a very good restaurant. At the time of our visits, L'Epicureo was owned by Tom and Rozann Buckner, who started on Federal Hill fifteen years ago in the space now occupied by Siena. L'Epicureo has always presented the highest quality food and the most careful presentation. Rozann comes from a long line of food folk; her late father owned the premiere butcher shop in the state. We began a recent meal with an amuse bouche of leek and potato soup with caramelized onion, which was a harbinger of the good meal to come. An appetizer of cauliflower and chestnut soup with caramelized onion and black truffles was thick and sumptuous; a Caesar salad lacked punch, but the seafood risotto was rich and balanced. The veal shank is the best in town and the chef's preparation of osso buco with risotto Milanese is probably the most succulent rendition of this dish anywhere. We are not sure why osso buco commands the same price on this menu ($34) as beef tenderloin, given that the veal shank is a far cheaper cut, but perhaps it is their signature dish. Pasta with veal Bolognese is $18, and fettucine carbonara a bit less. You can order half portions of pasta dishes, and all of the entrees are enticing and well presented.

We do want to warn you against going for dinner during pre-theatre hours, unless you are heading to a play. We went at 6:30 p.m. when PPAC featured a Broadway show, and we waited a half hour for a drink as theatergoers were ordering dessert and paying bills. Unfortunately, the waitstaff was also short one person that evening, but we would guess that when PPAC runs a show, it's better to go at 7:30 when the theatergoers have all left.

The Hotel Providence assumed ownership of L'Epicureo (with the Buckners heading off to embark on a new restaurant) in February 2008, but retained the same staff and chef. If the Buckners' high standards are maintained, L'Epicureo will continue to offer some of the best food in the city.

46. LJ's Barbecue

727 East Avenue (Hope Street)
Pawtucket, RI 02860
401-305-5255
www.ljsbbq.com
Lunch, Dinner daily
Brunch on weekends
$-$$

Yes, it's in Pawtucket, but it's like 15 feet over the line. And you should know about it. The minute you open the door at LJ's Barbecue, you know you've come to the right place. The sweet-smoky, porky aroma – really one of the top five smells – hits you right away and gets those gastric juices flowing freely. And once you sit down with the menu, and a beer from LJ's extensive and compelling beer list, your happiness will rise as fast as your anticipation. Only indecision will cloud your bliss.

And it's tough to choose, especially if it's your first visit. Everything on the menu looks so good, and the fragrance is sharpening your impatience. Let us save you the agony of choice: order "Award Winning BBQ St, Louis Style Ribs." Tender, juicy, smoky, with just the right amount of tangy sauce sticking to them. You can get a half-rack or a whole one, and a half is plenty for one normal person. Order the whole rack if you're planning to share. The dinner comes with two sides, or order a la carte and pick as many or as few sides as you want. LJ's offers regular sides, free with the dinner option, and premium sides, which cost a little extra. The regulars include cole slaw, macaroni salad, potato salad and barbecue beans. Among the premium sides, the macaroni and cheese and the collard greens are especially tasty and appropriate.

If for some reason a rack of ribs doesn't appeal, or just sounds like too much, try a pulled pork sandwich. Messy and delicious. All the sandwiches come with either a side or fries, and LJ's offers a large assortment. The burger at LJ's is also quite exceptional, but it's hard to not order the ribs.

Service at LJ's is friendly, accommodating, and low-key. For dates, for nights out with the family, or for an after-the-movies treat, we can't think of anything nicer than a plate of ribs and a beer at LJ's. And the price is right, too.

47. Local 121

121 Washington Street (Downcity)
Providence, RI 02903
401-274-2121
www.local121.com
Lunch, Dinner Monday-Saturday
Dinner Sunday
Reservations
$$$

Local 121 is serious. On Washington Street, this ambitious place lets you know even before you've seen the menu that it means business. The subdued, elegant-but-intimate setting is not what you expect of a place that is making its rep on food and wine from local fields, streams and vineyards. Where are the rustic touches, the primitive/outsider artworks, the mismatched tableware and jelly-jar glasses? For that matter, where are the pious sustainability sermons from menu or wait staff or both?

Local 121 preaches with its food: Bomster scallops from

Stonington, hangar steak from Maine, pork shank braised in Vidal Blanc from Sakonnet Vineyards. Greens will be increasingly local as the spring moves into summer. Yes, the place advertises itself as providing "locally harvested food and drink," but they don't beat you up with it. Prices are surprisingly realistic, given the luxe atmosphere; most main courses are at or below $20.

Have a burger – it's allowed, even encouraged. The meat is flavorful and perfectly cooked, on a big (too big, in our view) bun with excellent fries.

Wines by the glass are not surprising but are well-priced, with all selections below $10. On our last visit, only one was local (Sakonnet Eye of the Storm White Zinfandel, $5.50).

The room looks a bit like the dining room of a small, very exclusive hotel – which it is, in a way. It's at the old Dreyfus, now a new boutique inn on Washington. At two corners are round banquette alcoves, very plush, very romantic. Big drum-shaped lighting fixtures send soft flattering light off the dusty-gold ceiling and around the room strategically placed mirrors make the place look a little larger yet cozy at the same time. You will look your very best at Local 121.

Service is way better than average. Staff is very personable and well informed about the menu while details like keeping water glasses filled are responsibly handled.

Local 121 is one of the very best fine dining places in town. Big steakhouse chains are making a play here for the high end, but you can, in fact, have a very high-end experience right here, support a local business, and not spend half so much as you might elsewhere. Give it a shot.

48. Loie Fuller

1455 Westminster Street (West End)
Providence RI 02903
401-273-4375
Dinner Tuesday – Saturday
$$

Loie Fuller is one of those places you kind of discover, through word of mouth, blogs, or a friend who went there. (This place does little to announce itself.) Although it seems far away, because there are not many eateries on Upper Westminster Street, its location is almost parallel to the restaurants we frequent deeper on Broadway and Atwells Avenue. And then, in this small one story building, behind a very modest façade, you enter a tiny space which is utterly gorgeous. The dark woods, art deco paneling, walls painted in the style of Klimt, a busy bar, and a lovely dining room with a blazing fire will surprise and capture you. The menu is enticing, and the prices modest.

Loie Fuller offers a fine selection of wines, and when the chef is on his game, the food is delicious, even inspired, with a salad of beets. celeriac and goat cheese, served warm with a champagne vinaigrette, or a dish of Kurobuta pork cheeks braised in red wine and served over apple-flecked risotto. You can enjoy a very pleasant evening with cocktails and wine for under $75 a couple, including tip. It's fair to say that we've had some misses from the kitchen, but we still love the place. We'd love it for the artistry alone, but we also appreciate the intent: an imaginative menu, affordable wines, superb service, and some very good food.

49. McCormick and Schmick

11 Dorrance Street (Downcity)
Providence RI 02903
401-351-4500
www.mccormickandschmick.com
Breakfast, Lunch, Dinner daily
Reservations
$$$-$$$$

There was a time not too long ago when you had to take a trip to McCormick & Schmick's Seafood Restaurant in Seattle or Portland to experience the seafood of the Pacific Northwest. Copper River Alaskan King salmon, when in season, was the best eating imaginable: the fish was perfectly grilled, the slight crunch of the lightly charred top yielding to the incredibly fresh, buttery taste of the meat below was a huge success.

Now the chain has a branch in founder Bill McCormick's home town and the seafood is still top-notch, although the atmosphere has become rather generic. When you enter from the lobby of the Biltmore Hotel, you might think you're in just another hotel dining room. The dark paneling, forest green walls and tasteful but unsurprisingly men's-grill look of the place could be anywhere.

But when you settle in with the menu you'll see "Fresh List" at the top. That's everything that's fresh that day. Happily, the list is extensive and includes nice plump, briny clams and oysters from our local waters. See what they have – quahogs or littlenecks and Chatham or Fishers Island oysters are a great way to jump-start a meal here.

Seafood specialties start at about $17.50 and may include very rare seared yellowfin tuna served with a chilled Asian cucumber salad and Georges Bank scallops served with prosciutto, mushrooms and asiago cheese. Of course, if Alaskan Copper River King salmon is available, order it. (The season usually starts in mid-May.) You may be in Providence, but McCormick & Schmick's can transport you to the scenic shores of Puget Sound. This fish is so superior to Atlantic, let alone farmed, salmon, it should get a new name. The flavor is delicate yet emphatically oceanic and the texture meltingly tender.

We should mention that McCormick & Schmick's features one of the best food bargains anywhere with its $1.95 bar menu. From 3:30-6:30 PM and from 10 PM to midnight, you can choose from these selections: a half-pound cheeseburger with fries, potato croquettes, spinach and artichoke dip with tortilla chips, cheese quesadilla, seafood nachos, or steamed mussels in white wine and garlic broth…all from $1.95. If there's a better deal anywhere, we'd love to hear about it.

Providence, a seaport city, has surprisingly few places where you can satisfy your seafood craving. Although Hemenway's is certainly the most successful homegrown establishment, let's not forget that the McCormick in McCormick & Schmick is a Providence native. We're lucky he brought his winning way with seafood back home.

50. Mediterraneo

134 Atwells Avenue (Federal Hill)
Providence RI 02903
401-331-7760
www.mediterraneocaffe.com
Lunch Monday-Saturday
Dinner nightly
Reservations
$$$-$$$$

Mediterraneo has an air of glamour about it. Whether it's the gold leaf on the walls, or the large French doors that always seem to be filled with diners, or the regular celebrity sightings, Mediterraneo oozes energy and sex appeal. The crowd spills on to the sidewalk in the summer, and it was *the* spot to see Buddy in the old days. Driving by the busy cafe always makes you wonder why you aren't sitting there yourself.

The food is classic Italian, with a never changing menu, but it's done right. Mediterraneo has a sensational antipasto. One of our favorite appetizers is the crostini con portabella e manzo, which is a blend of tenderloin tips and portabella mushrooms in a creamy sauce fragrant with Madeira wine. The chef prepares tagliatelle Bolognese, spinach canelloni, and spaghetti alla vongole (with clams, white wine, and garlic) in their traditional forms. On the entrée list, the grilled ahi tuna served over cannellini beans topped with eggplant caponata and grilled chicken breast marinated in balsamic vinegar and olive oil are as popular as the pork or seafood or beef dishes. The menu never changes because the customers demand these dishes again and again.

Mediterraneo offers three pages of wines to choose from with four reds and four whites by the glass at an affordable $7 price. Summer or winter, lunch or dinner, Mediterraneo is an appealing option.

51. Mill's Tavern

101 North Main Street (College Hill)
Providence, RI 02903
401-272-3331
www.millstAvenuernrestaurant.com
Dinner nightly
Reservations
$$$

Mill's Tavern is both timeless and cutting edge. The interior space is utterly handsome with innumerable noteworthy touches, like the handblown seeded glass lanterns, and the Tom Sgouros paintings that change seasonally over the bar, the Coral Bourgeois mosaic tiles that line the walls, the blacksmith's leather booths, the spotless gleaming open kitchen, the dark long big-backed bar, and the chef's table made of a single 3" thick piece of California Oak. Mill's is a monument to craftsmanship and artistry. It is also a first-rate restaurant overseen by the now iconic Providence restaurateur Jaime D'Oliveira.

The menu offers a raw bar, which is a rare option these days. You'll find the freshest oysters and littlenecks on the half shell as well as crab claws with a mustard remoulade. Extra large shrimp are poached to perfection in a flavorful broth, and then chilled on ice. From the pantry, the menu offers Portugal's great contribution to Rhode Island eating: native littleneck clams dotted with grilled chorizo and sweet onions, braised in a spicy tomato and Sagres beer broth. The rabbit ravioli served open-faced with wild mushrooms includes sage and a hint of truffles. From the wood burning oven come Port braised short ribs and rack of lamb. A wood-fired rotisserie produces a succulent buttermilk marinated chicken, and Mill's serves excellent prime steaks and chops cooked to perfection on the wood-fired grill.

Year after year, Mill's has won award after award and has never relaxed its high standards for food and service. We recommend Mill's with no hesitation for its inviting ambience, its impressive wine list, and its consistently excellent food. Its beautiful private dining room seats up to 20. Prices range from $19 for chicken to $40 for the prime steak. Wines by the glass run about $8-$9.

52. MuMu Cuisine
220 Atwells Avenue (Federal Hill)
Providence, RI 02903
401-369-7040
Lunch, Dinner daily
Reservations
$$

In 2006, a sophisticated contemporary Chinese restaurant opened in the heart of Providence's Italian neighborhood. Sophia Cuyegkeng opened MuMu Cuisine with the goal of operating a restaurant that serves authentic Chinese food, rather than the Americanized version. To that end, Sophia brought in Chef Lao Sun who cooked in Beijing for the top government officials in China. Sophia and Chef Sun have created an extensive menu which showcases familiar and new dishes, all freshly prepared and offered at reasonable prices.

Chef Sun serves the traditional Peking Ravioli, but he also offers Xiao Long Bao, commonly known as the "soupy dumpling". It is an extraordinary delicacy, with steamed dumplings that contain minced vegetables and meat in a flavorful broth. The first bite is a shot of soup, and then the fragrant filling follows; instructions even come with the dish. Other appetizers include a sensational crab Rangoon and crisp scallion pancakes. The popular General Tso's Chicken is on the menu, but a more unusual dish called crispy beef, contains succulent strips of julienned beef with thin breading which gives it crunch; its accompanying spicy sauce finishes the dish perfectly. MuMu Cuisine features Peking duck daily with a choice of a half or a whole duck. Among the seafood entrées is a whole steamed sea bass with fresh ginger and scallions, a delicate scallop dish sautéed with assorted vegetables and prawns in a silky cream sauce with walnuts.

MuMu Cuisine is handsomely decorated with tangerine walls and black paneling. The lighting is soft and the ambience is distinctly appealing suitable equally for a romantic evening, a quiet dinner, or a family gathering. There is a full bar and valet parking.

53. Napa Valley Grille

111 Providence Place (Downcity)
Providence RI 02903
401-270-6272
www.napavalleygrille.com
Lunch, Dinner – daily
Reservations
$$$

Napa Valley Grille is surprisingly good for a chain restaurant in a mall. It offers excellent food and superb wines by the glass. The cuisine is described as "wine country," and the wine list is nationally recognized as one of the best and most extensive in the United States. For years, it has attracted significant chefs who create appealing menus and notable food. One of the best choices in years is a duck confit in a demi-glace atop corn bread, rich and sweet and savory all at once. The hamburger is as good as anyone else's in the city, and if you are exhausted from shopping or if you are dining before a Rhode Island Philharmonic concert at Veterans Memorial Auditorium, a quick dinner in the Napa Valley bar will satisfy you perfectly.

Many booths provide comfortable dining, the staff manages to make a cavernous dining room cozy by curtaining off part of it when it is empty. Sitting cityside in the bar area is also attractive with a glittering view of the State House or the train station. The other Napa Valley Grilles are in impressive locales, like Yountville and San Diego, California so we feel lucky that Providence is a chosen destination. The menus reflect the best in New American and cuisine changes according to seasons and availability of local produce.

This one gets the nod with its casual elegant surroundings, gracious service and tasty cuisine.

54. New Rivers

7 Steeple Street (College Hill)
Providence RI 02903
401-751-0350
www.newriversrestaurant.com
Dinner Monday-Saturday
Reservations
$$$-$$$$

In the 18 years that New Rivers has been operating, owner Bruce Tillinghast and his chef de cuisine, Beau Vestal, have so finely tuned their food that each appetizer and entrée actually startles you into recognition of your experience. When you add that to the lovely ambience, a terrific bartender and great service, your evening is sublime.

Begin the evening with a perfect cocktail, like a Cosmopolitan, the twist and the fresh lime juice make such a difference that you wonder why most bartenders cannot master this drink. Take time to notice the tasteful, soothing surroundings: forest green and crimson walls, several cozy booths, and small tables each with one perfect flower. Listen as your informed yet unobtrusive waiter explains the creative and amazing menu and relax with the knowledge that you will have superb food.

Tillinghast was the first chef in Providence to champion local seasonal products, and his sensitivity to their qualities is what makes the food so extraordinary. Other than a lemon tartlet and a praline ice cream, the menu at New Rivers changes seasonally and continually. Whether it is rosemary-infused gnocchi with Tuscan sausage, or venison served atop turnips and Brussels sprouts, or a caramelized, crunchy apple crisp, the chef prepares the food with an eye to coaxing the maximum flavor from each ingredient. Three white and three red wines choices by the glass cost between $8 and $10. A wine list of about 120 wines is mostly American but does include European and New World wines from Australia, New Zealand and South America, with prices ranging from $22 a bottle to $210.

New Rivers has won many many awards since it opened and the modest, gracious Tillinghast is among the most admired and beloved people on the RI scene. Try New Rivers and you will understand why his attention to detail keeps him at the top.

55. Nicks on Broadway

500 Broadway (West End)
Providence RI 02909
401-421-0286
www.nicksonbroadway.com
Breakfast, Lunch Wednesday - Sunday
Dinner, Wednesday - Saturday
Reservations Dinner only
$$-$$$

Nicks on Broadway will make our top ten list no matter which of us is speaking. (Or writing.) It is the creation of its owner-chef, Derek Wagner, who hit the scene running five years ago when he opened up a tiny diner on Broadway, serving breakfast and lunch. His restaurant was so popular that it was only a matter of time before he had to expand. Recently, Wagner moved into a stunning new space with 40 seats, added dinner to his repertoire, and got a liquor license. The place has a sleek, functional, stylish look, with bright red tiles providing the contrast to the slate gray walls and tables. A sparkling stainless steel open kitchen faces the dining room and produces remarkable food. Broadway is Providence's version of Manhattan's SoHo, and the ambience at Nicks perfectly suits the neighborhood. It also perfectly suits Wagner's approach to food. His menu is smart, contemporary, fresh, simple and understated. He calls it a modern take on rustic French country cooking, with a splash of Mediterranean influence.

Open for all three meals, Nicks offers a menu at breakfast that is just as interesting as the one at lunch and dinner. The place is always hopping. Nicks boasts moderate prices, artisan beers, and terrific wines by the glass for about $6. His dinner menu features a specialty game sausage, which changes regularly from lamb to boar, duck to veal, but it is always served in a rich brown sauce which perfectly complements the meat. The food is always fresh and seasonal, so that entrées on the fall menu might include roasted sea scallops with a butternut squash potato puree and a cider reduction or a grilled fall-spiced boneless duck with pumpkin polenta and apple jus. A nightly special offers slices of venison with a sauté of wild mushrooms, four vegetables and red wine jus. The desserts are sensational and shouldn't be missed even if you are stuffed from dinner. Warm pumpkin bread pudding with caramel and vanilla ice cream, or a lime scented pound cake with whipped cream and lime zest, vie for your attention, as well as a warm dark chocolate fudge brownie topped with fresh whipped cream and fruit compote. You choose. It's not easy.

We should definitely add that the service at Nicks is first rate. Our waiter, Steve, remembered what four of us had chosen to eat and six weeks after our first visit! That makes anyone feel pretty special. Make your reservation soon!

56. Oak

959 Hope Street (Hope Street)
Providence, RI 02906
401-273-7275
Lunch, Dinner Tuesday-Sunday
Brunch on weekends
Reservations for 6 or more
$$

You have to like Oak. It's not trying to prove anything. It just wants to give you a good meal that's more interesting than plain old comfort food, but isn't gussied up. And Oak delivers.

The room is attractive. Sienna walls and furnishings create a warm atmosphere, and the tables are nicely spaced so you don't have to listen to your neighbor argue with her decorator. At lunch there's an interesting sandwich selection plus a daily soup, which is usually delicious. Main courses include choices like Maine crab cakes with sweet potato fries ($13) and meat loaf with caramelized onion gravy and mashed potatoes ($10). The Angus burger with sautéed mushrooms, cheddar, bacon and Dijon mayo is pretty great, too ($9.00). "Big lobster ravioli" with grilled shrimp, tomato confit and roasted leeks ($20) headlines the pasta choices, and you can always get linguine with clams. At dinner, the menu continues to tantalize with appetizers like crispy pasta-wrapped garlic and leek custard with asparagus and Hollandaise sauce. Among the dinner entrees, the priciest item is a hanger steak au poivre with blue cheese potato gratin and Port wine sauce for $23.

The service is professional and friendly, and the staff remembers you at Oak. The cocktails are expertly mixed and the wine list is extremely friendly and affordable.

On Sunday nights, Oak serves a three-course dinner for two with wine for $20. Service is friendly and prompt, and the food is fresh, well-prepared and interesting enough to keep you coming back. What's not to like?

57. Old Canteen

120 Atwells Avenue (Federal Hill)
Providence, RI 02903
Phone: (401) 751-5544
Lunch, Dinner Closed Tuesday
Reservations
$$-$$$

If you're over 40 and you're looking for a spot that will show your ravaged complexion in the most flattering possible light, reserve a table now at The Old Canteen. It's pink in there – a pink that may have faded from the Sherwin-Williams catalog, but not from the walls of this Providence classic. Opened in 1956, and still officially known to many as Joe Marzilli's Old Canteen, because of its late venerable owner, it is probably safe to say that not much has changed: not the décor, and not the menu, which is long on the ample tried and true: spaghetti with clams; chicken, veal, and eggplant parmigiana; scampi fra diavolo; manicotti, lasagna. The full dinner menu includes appetizer, salad and dessert.

But once in the rather formal (you half-expect Ike and Mamie to walk in, escorted by Frank and Dino) dining room, you'll find that even if the printed menu can't, your very pleasant and knowledgeable server can, in fact, surprise you. Often the specials depart from the rote traditions of the menu and show real flair and creativity. Recently an eggplant roulade blew us away. The thin slices of eggplant had been dipped in flour and egg and quickly fried. Next each slice was wrapped around a filling of ground beef, ricotta, pine nuts, then baked in a robe of béchamel with enriched with gorgonzola. The result was light (really!) and delicate, with the taste of gorgonzola coming in at the end of each bite and literally changing the flavors in your mouth.

For years diners have been coming to The Old Canteen regularly, sometimes once a week, and sometimes for special occasions. Sometimes Providencians take visitors here for a glimpse of the old days, when Joe Marzilli's place was one of the few serious restaurants in town. It's still a serious restaurant. Joe's son is the chef now (he has been for years), and he is clearly capable of preparing interesting, delicious food. Drop by and ask your server about the specials. Then check out your fellow diners. Doesn't everyone look marvelous?

58. Olga's Cup and Saucer

103 Point Street (Downcity)
Providence, RI 02903
401-831-6666
www.olgascupandsaucer.com
Breakfast and Lunch Monday-Saturday
Brunch on Saturday
$$

Olga Bravo is one of those Providence artists who has brought her creative talent to the food world. Her little restaurant on Point Street is loaded with charm and atmosphere and in the summer deserves that hackneyed title of "oasis" with its shady, lovely garden seating.

Olga is a baker by trade and so good that she supplies many of the high end restaurants here with her artisan baguettes, olive loafs, croissants and other delicious breads. She is also a talented and inventive chef creating hearty and satisfying soups. Her salads, such as the Mayan chicken salad or the Thai noodle salad, are flavorful and interesting. Try her little pizzas; they are addictive. The gooey spinach and goat cheese calzone is so good you cannot think about the calories. Olga's is a great spot for breakfast or a cup of coffee, but you probably can't get a better lunch anywhere. If you get lunch at Olga's with a salad or pizza and beverage, you're probably going to spend about twelve dollars. If you add that tempting pastry, you will spend a little more, but you may not be able to resist it.

Olga's is a casual, comfortable place, and we have been back again and again.

59. Opa

244 Atwells Ave (Federal Hll)
Providence, RI 02903
(401) 351-8282
Reservations
Dinner nightly, Brunch Sunday in the summer
$$-$$$

Is Opa the best Lebanese restaurant in Providence? Until our attention is called to another one, we have to say so. Lebanese cooking is in the eastern Mediterranean tradition most familiar to us through Greek food. The cuisine was spread throughout the region by the Ottoman Turks, who used to rule everything in sight. What distinguishes the Lebanese variety from the

Greek is more use of Middle Eastern spices and ingredients. But there are ubiquitous dishes – stuffed grape leaves, tabbouleh, hummus, and kabobs – that will insure that you feel at home when you visit Opa.

Salads are a major feature here. They're generous, and they're good. The Salad Opa ($12 at dinner) is loaded with shrimp, calamari, salmon and scallops in an olive oil and cilantro dressing. It is wildly popular. An equally popular dish is the hummus ($7) prepared with garlic, olive oil and tahini, and served with toasted pita points; it is tempting to settle down with just that crisp bread and creamy, mouth-filling spread and make a night of it. One of the restaurant's reasonably priced wines would round out the evening.

But in the event that you want to move beyond hummus, Mediterranean pasta ($13) is an option. It's basically spaghetti aglio olio, with the addition of feta. For a few dollars more, you can add seafood to the dish. Opa offers a variety of seafood choices, from calamari to scallops and salmon. Grilled seafood Opa ($19) delivers a mix of all of the above, served on a bed of rice.

If you're expecting a night of middle Eastern authenticity, you can choose the meze. At dinner, for $35 per person, a minimum of two people can enjoy a 12-dish selection of Lebanese meze, or small dishes, selected by the chef. Or you can call ahead and request special dishes not on the menu. If it's an evening of Levantine culinary excitement you seek, this would be our recommendation. The standard Opa menu is geared to a diner who's not looking for the unfamiliar: lots of pastas, salads, grilled fish – and even spaghetti with meatballs!

Opa is a friendly, low-voltage little place that aims to please, and generally does. It would be nice to see a few more Lebanese offerings on the menu.

60. Pakarang

303 South Main Street (Fox Point)
Providence RI 02903
401-453-3660
www.PakarangRestaurant.com
Lunch Tuesday - Saturday
Dinner nightly
$$

When Pakarang opened on South Main Street about 13 years ago, it was ahead of the Providence palate. Thai food hadn't really made inroads into Rhode Island. But now we are more seasoned connoisseurs of ethnic cuisine, and Thai food is both popular and appreciated. This serene space serves an extensive array of Thai dishes from satay to pad thai in an easily decipherable menu. It has been Americanized so that Tom Kaa soup is referred to as chicken coconut soup, which by any name is a light fragrant broth of coconut and vegetables with a choice of chicken or seafood. The Pakarang version is mild and soothing.

The menu separates the entrées into sections of appealing curries, salads, appetizers, soups and main dishes, each with a symbolic number of chile peppers representing the degree of heat. We sampled a pleasing pad thai (no peppers) and a sautéed beef and basil with the two peppers graphic (indicating hot and spicy.) This particular beef dish included onions, peppers, string beans, and mushrooms in a garlicky sweet and spicy sauce. The spice factor to our taste was only mild, and again perhaps Americanized. We have eaten in Thai restaurants where they believed our courageous word, and we could barely inhale for the fire on our tongues.

Pakarang is fancier than Sawadee, and slightly more expensive, but it has a similar menu in an attractive space and includes a full bar. When you want your Thai food with ambience, Pakarang is where you will be happiest.

61. Pane e Vino

365 Atwells Avenue (Federal Hill)
Providence RI 02903
401-223-2230
www.panevino.com
Dinner nightly
Reservations
$$$

Pane e Vino is one of our favorite spots on the hill. The food is rustic and authentic. Owner Joe De Quattro, who also owns Zooma, and used to own Caffe Itri, knows his wines well and presents an impressive list. Dinner always includes at least one wonderful discovery that we want to have again or at least recreate. Pane e Vino is inviting, whether you are seated at the front by the windows facing Atwells Avenue, or in one of the booths along the wall. A back room that is a little bit quieter features a gas fireplace and is ideal for parties or an intimate dinner. The configuration of the restaurant lends a special feeling to each section. The walls, which are sponged the color of a Mediterranean sunset, add to the overall good feeling.

The restaurant bustles because it offers extremely flavorful food, like a pasta with sausage and marinara sauce that adds a bit of beef broth to the marinara, yielding a richer, deeper taste. A grilled piece of Scamorza cheese bathed in a light marinara sauce is a particular hit from the appetizer list. Many seafood antipasti choices include white anchovies and spicy chili peppers with fresh lemon juice and extra virgin olive oil. The pasta choices and entrees reflect the cooking of Southern Italy, straightforward, relying on fresh ingredients and simple preparation. Risotto ai frutti di mare features scallops, octopus, mussels, clams, shrimp and calamari. The rice is carnaroli, not the plebian arborio. You know you're moving up in the world when your risotto is made with carnaroli rice. Chef prepares a thick veal chop ($33) pounded thin, breaded lightly and then served with marinara and mozzarella.

The extensive wine list ranges from simple Stracalli Chianti for $22 a bottle to an Antonelli Solaia for $265. Dozens of wines are available by the glass.

62. Paragon

234 Thayer Street (College Hill)
Providence, RI 02906
401-331-6200
www.vivaparagon.com
Lunch, Dinner, Brunch on weekends
$$
Reservations for 6 more

Fabulous burgers, great fries, cozy surroundings, consistently good food and service make Paragon one of Providence's most popular restaurants. In the heart of the Brown campus, it has long been crowded with students, professors and East Siders. It manages to be one cut above a burger joint, even though it is arguably the best burger joint in town. Paragon has a selection of about five terrific salads, a bargain $19 sirloin with garlic butter, fish entrees including fresh haddock, salmon and ahi tuna among other choices. Paragon basically offers a solid menu that manages to cover every taste, including the family vegetarians. The bar mixes great Cosmopolitans and Planters Punch and offers a good selection of wines by the glass, which run from $5 to $7.75.

Paragon is one of those places that people hit once or twice a week to meet for lunch with friends, or have an affordable dinner that tastes great and doesn't break the bank.

63. Parkside

76 South Main Street (College Hill)
Providence, RI 02903
401-331-0003
www.parksideprovidence.com
Lunch, Dinner daily
Reservations
$$-$$$

Parkside has found a successful niche in the Providence scene. Owner and Chef Steve Davenport and his wife have run it since 1996, and there is rarely a night when the place isn't bustling. The bar is and always has been a popular watering hole. The location, across from the river, makes it a perfect spot for WaterFire dining. The large iron French rotisserie, carefully tended by friendly sous-chefs, produces impeccably crisp and juicy chicken, as well as duck and tenderloin, and even desserts. We know some patrons who go there just for the fresh fish or the sliced tenderloin atop a perfect spring mix salad.

The energy in this restaurant provides a warm and chic feeling, like a busy bistro on Manhattan's East Side. Steve Davenport offers basic New American cuisine, prepared well. He runs a tight, efficient, warm and friendly ship, and when we go to Parkside, we always know we'll have a good meal, and we are never disappointed. The wait staff is friendly, efficient and loyal; indeed, many faces have been there since it opened.

Try the spicy crabcakes, or the veal and sage agnolotti. If you're tempted by the pan-roasted Chatham cod, served over a French lentil stew with pancetta, caramelized carrots and morel mushrooms, topped with wilted spinach, go for it. But at some point, and it may be many meals later, you must try the lemon and garlic chicken, with the zippy green sauce, or rotisserie cashew chicken. Either way, you will lick every sticky remnant from your fingers. We promise.

64. Phonatic

165 Angell Street (College Hill)
Providence RI 02906
401-454-1699
Lunch and Dinner daily, BYOB
$-$$

Located in the midst of the Brown campus, Phonatic took over Asian Paradise and it now serves delicate well-prepared

Vietnamese dishes. It is possible, therefore, to grab a soothing bowl of pho on a daily basis right on the East Side. Pho is the Vietnamese soup that features a deep and flavorful broth, fresh rice noodles, and an accent of all fresh ingredients: basil, limes, jalapenos, and bamboo shoots. It's the freshness that makes you return for more. Good pho is the perfect antidote to what ails you and Phonatic makes good pho. For $6.50, two people can share the small version as an appetizer. One of the most appealing lunch offerings is a crisp salad of cabbage, shredded carrots and onions, tossed in a lime dressing, and topped with roasted peanuts and fried shallot flakes. This salad, which costs $7.95, can include chicken or shrimp, beef or lotus stems. A scattering of fresh mint leaves in the salad makes the overall taste even more refreshing.

The extensive menu at Phonatic, with over 100 choices, offers classic Vietnamese flavors and ingredients. The Bo Nhung Dam special is a hot pot you dip lightly seasoned beef into warm rice vinegar stock and then wrap the beef in rice paper along with steamed rice vermicelli and vegetables.

Phonatic overlooks Angell Street in a simple but pleasant dining room that can accommodate about 75 diners. It is the new sister of Pho Paradise. There is no bar, but it is certainly acceptable to bring your own beer or wine. Most dishes are under $10, with the exception of some of the specials. All the portions seem ample and easy to share. Service is attentive and polite.

65. Pho Paradise
337 Broad Street (West End)
Providence, RI 02903
401-369-7990
Lunch, Dinner daily
Reservations
$

It's easy to make fun of the name of this place, but there's nothing faux about the food. This tastes and feels like real Vietnamese cooking, in the kind of mini-strip mall setting that somehow seems authentic.

Pho, of course, is the classic noodle soup dish that may be the ultimate meal in a bowl. But there's more to Pho Paradise than noodles. When you take your seat in the brightly lighted, no-frills dining room, you receive a menu that is long, bewildering, and frequently as indecipherable as the Nag Hammadi codices. But your server is helpful and patient, and soon you will happily sample some of the tastiest food in Providence.

The summer roll appetizer is a cool rice-flour cylinder of slivered vegetables and pork or shrimp, served with a peanut dipping sauce. Light and just spicy enough to be interesting, it is also quite beautiful on the plate, where it doesn't stay long. Scallion pancakes are also delicious and oddly irresistible. Your brain says "enough already," but your hand keeps stuffing more in your mouth.

A wide variety of Phos is available, and some of the menu descriptions may fall into the "too much information" category. The featured Pho is beef, in a number of sizes and, well, shapes. You may find it useful to know that one beef Pho contains tendon as well as tripe, but then again, if you've never had tendon, maybe you should try it. If you do, you'll find it somewhat springy and not at all bad. It's more a texture than a taste experience. The Pho itself is a tasty broth with wonderful, soft, slurpy noodles, lots of beef bits including thin slices of ribeye, and a beautiful side plate with bean sprouts, mint leaves and chilis to add to taste. Everything is good, and everything you add makes it better. There are also some non-beef Phos, including chicken and shrimp. The chicken soup would comfort you on any cold winter day or cure what ails you just about any time.

If you're an experienced consumer of Vietnamese food, you will find plenty of non-Pho options to explore. If you're not, Pho Paradise is a great place to begin your discovery of this marvelous, sophisticated, elegant cuisine.

66. Pizzico

762 Hope Street (Hope Street)
Providence, RI 02906
401-421-4114
www.pizzicoprori.com
Lunch and Dinner
Reservations
$$$

What on earth is Pizzico doing on Hope Street? Inquiring minds want to know. It feels as if it belongs on Atwells Avenue. It looks that way, too, with an authentic little-Italy glimmery allure. Most of all, the food would be right at home on Federal Hill. Get past the rather ordinary storefront façade and you find yourself in a comfortable, welcoming place that will satisfy your cravings – for crispy thin-crust 8" pizzas ($9.95 for the Margherita), pasta like strozzapreti with lamb sausage (17.95), sogliola cuocopazzo (sole with a pistachio & horseradish crust, $18.95) or cioppino ($25.95), the seafood stew that made San Francisco famous. Or maybe it was vice-versa. The menu offers so many appealing choices that even on those occasions when you've walked in with a craving for pasta, you can end up ordering scottaditta balsamico ($28.95) instead. (Your wallet may be lighter, but you won't be.)

Pizzico boasts one of the biggest and best wine lists in Providence, so you can knock yourself out with a super-Tuscan for your scottaditta, or find a fruity and reasonably priced Primitivo to go with your pizza and salad.

Pizzico's counter-intuitive location has many advantages. You can drive up Hope Street and park easily, unlike the dodgem-car scene on Atwells Avenue. It's not as big a scene as some of the Federal Hill spots, and it has a cozy neighborhood vibe. But it's definitely not a fallback. The food is authentic, flavorful and satisfying. After just one visit, you'll add it to your Favorites List.

67. Pot au Feu

4 Custom House Street (Downcity)
Providence 02903
401-273-8953
www.potaufeuri.com
Lunch Monday-Friday
Dinner nightly
Reservations
$$-$$$

Owner Bob Burke, along with Al Forno's George Germon and Johanne Killeen, brought fine dining to Providence over a quarter-century ago. Both places continue to prosper, and for good reasons: good food and consistency. Pot au Feu also benefits from Bob's welcoming, gregarious presence at the door. He seems to know all the diners by name, and they greet each other like old friends. Perhaps they are.

Pot au Feu has an upstairs, downstairs attribute that makes it possible to enjoy an elegant, classic French meal upstairs in the Salon, or a casual, bistro-style one downstairs. In both venues, you will dine on carefully and authentically prepared food, and find the service friendly and attentive. In between greeting guests at the door, Bob circulates, to make sure you're happy as well as to offer menu suggestions for the undecided.

Bouillabaisse ($23.95) and, yes, pot-au-feu ($22.95) are both authentic and delicious. On a cold winter's night in Providence, nothing could be finer than to settle in down in the bistro and slurp up a big bowl of fresh seafood in a fragrant, garlic-and-saffron broth, or a meaty, soul-satisfying pot-au-feu. The onion soup is perfectly seasoned and bubbly, and the sautéed chicken livers remain a favorite for folks who go there frequently just for those dishes. Add the crusty bread, a bottle of Muscadet ($23) or Moulin-a-Vent ($33), and we challenge you to be unhappy. In the Salon, "Suprême de Caneton et Confit de Gigot Bigarade" is a dependable crowd-pleaser: duck breast and duck leg confit with an orange sauce ($26).

In the case of Pot au Feu, longevity has not meant complacency. The place works hard to win and retain its guests and never takes them for granted. The menu is tried and true - - you won't find culinary adventure here, but you will find a warm welcome and food that's true to its French traditions.

68. Providence Oyster Bar

283 Atwells Avenue (Federal Hill)
Providence RI 02904
401-272-8866
www.providenceoysterbar.com
Lunch Friday and Saturday
Dinner Monday -Saturday
Reservations
$$$

Right in the middle of the Atwells Avenue restaurant row, Providence Oyster Bar feels a bit like a fish out of water. Or an oyster. It has a polish and vibe that owes nothing to its neighbors, yet it adds variety and richness to the Atwells scene – by being different, and by being very good.

When you walk in, you see a raw bar right in front of you with a cluster of tables. A long handsome bar extends down the left-hand side of the restaurant and tables run down the right side. The place is done in dark woods and muted lighting and has a steakhouse kind of feel very different from the traditional buoys-and-fishing-nets design concept common to New England seafood spots.

If you're fond of oysters (and why would you be here if you're not?), you'll find a good choice of local and imported bivalves. They're shucked to order and invariably fresh, cold and briny, served with a piquant mignonette sauce. Littleneck and cherrystone clams are also seashore fresh and come with the traditional cocktail sauce, which you can jazz up further with horseradish and/or Tabasco. Oysters are $2.35 each and clams are $1.75.

At dinner, one of the menu stars is the Block Island swordfish ($28.99), wrapped in prosciutto and served with truffle fries and grilled asparagus. There is also lobster and Alaskan King Crab ($19.99 for ½ pound, $35.99 for a pound). If for some reason you were brought here against your will, filet mignon ($36.99) and braised short rib ($22.99) options, beautifully prepared, should ease your pain. Fish and chips, at $19.99, are served with the restaurant's perfect long and thin French fries…ridiculously addictive.

Providence Oyster Bar boasts a well-selected and broad wine list and the wines by the glass are in the $7.00-$10.00 range. You will find interesting choices in every price bracket.

P.O.B. is the kind of place where it would be fun to watch the Super Bowl on the big flat-screen at the end of the bar while slurping down oysters and beer in an upscale yet totally unpretentious atmosphere. The food is excellent, while not inexpensive. In the evening there's valet parking, which on Atwells is virtually a requirement. Drive over there, let them park your car, and enjoy.

69. Providence Prime

279 Atwells Avenue (Federal Hill)
Providence, RI 02903
401-454-8881
www.providenceprime.com
Dinner Monday-Saturday
Reservations
$$$$

Bill Clinton eats here when he comes to Providence and after a number of visits, we don't wonder why. Prime has the upscale steakhouse look perfected. There's a nice long bar on the left as you enter, with a (thankfully muted) TV down at the end. The lighting is soft, and the décor has those woody, handsome but unsurprising men's-den tones that let you know that the people here understand you and your uncomplicated cravings. You want red meat and lots of it in a setting that doesn't distract you by calling attention to itself.

So they treat you as if you're prosperous, not decadent. If you choose, you can dine at the bar, where the bartender will introduce himself. Soon you and he discuss the wine list and the menu options like old acquaintances. He's well-informed but not a know-it-all, helpful but not intrusive.

The menu offers beef in most or all of the usual configurations --- New York strip, filet, and rib eye --- including the porterhouse for two, 38 ounces for $78. Two thick American loin lamb chops cost $32, and braised short ribs are $28. All the portions are generous, the meat is top-quality and gorgeously prepared. In classic steakhouse style, everything is a la carte, so your hunk o' burnin' protein arrives in front of you unadorned.

Among the sides the "fresh cut ribbon onion strings" could keep you coming back even if the rest of the food didn't floor you. Light, crisp, greaseless and full of sweet onion goodness, they are irresistible. Sautéed spinach is a good choice, preferable to the creamed spinach which does not come together as a dish – it seems to be cooked spinach that has then been immersed in cream. The flavors and textures never meld appropriately. If you're up to adding a dumpster-full of carbs to your protein allotment for the month, order the Cottage Fries. All the sides are large enough for two hearty eaters.

You don't really care about dessert, but you should definitely care about the wine list, which is thoughtful, comprehensive, and fairly priced. On a recent visit we noticed a 2002 D'Arenbourg Shiraz, "The Dead Arm," from McLaren Vale in Australia. It retails for as much as $90 a bottle, and Providence Prime has it for $95. If you're celebrating with steak or giant lamb chops, this is a perfect wine to help make it special. Extensive listings of Italian wines are also a strength of this exceptional collection.

Bring money and bring an appetite. While expensive, Providence Prime is not the priciest steakhouse you'll find, but as a member of that world, it offers good values. Service is professional as well as personable. Fast for a week or so, then check it out.

70. Ran Zan

1084 Hope Street (Hope Street)
Providence, RI 02906
401-276-7574
www.ranzan.net
Lunch, Dinner
Closed Monday
$$

Named after a country village in Japan, Ran Zan (pronounced "Ron Zon") offers scrupulously fresh sushi and sashimi, tempura, teriyaki, Japanese noodle soups, and yakisoba. No surprises – if you're familiar with most Japanese menus in Providence, the one at Ran Zan won't shock or awe you.

On that little strip where Blackstone Boulevard runs into the north end of Hope Street, this tiny spot (eight tables plus a five or six-seat sushi bar) almost bends over backwards not to raise your expectations too high. The hostess is friendly but not effusive. She waves you to a seat. If you choose the counter, the sushi chef does not look up from his work, nor does he bellow those hearty Japanese sushi chef greetings so popular elsewhere. He's busy.

He prepares some of the very best, most authentic sushi and sashimi in town. The assortment is not overwhelming. If you're a habitué of high-end sushi parlors in New York or Boston, you may find that esoteric specialties you favor are not on the menu. Toro tuna is listed, yet it is not always available. But when you make your selection, you will be happy.

Start with sashimi. An order is three pieces. Tuna comes in thick, compact slices, propped up on a bed of shredded daikon and a shiso leaf. It is positively fresh, and each piece is a perfect mouthful. Fluke comes as a flower-shaped roll of the three slices along with a slice of lemon and pickled ginger. The arrangement of the two selections on the small square plate is exquisite.

Try some sushi next. Uni ($4 for two pieces), or sea urchin, sits in its little seaweed wrap as it does everywhere --- but the wrap is still crispy (a condition that lasts about 15 seconds, so grab it right away), making a wonderful little texture contrast with the creamy, briny uni. Sea bass, yellowtail, eel – all are just right. Nothing showy, just delicious. The sushi offerings here, unlike so many, are sized so that you can pop each one into your mouth and experience the tastes and textures without feeling (and looking) as if you were trying to masticate a tennis ball.

Ran Zan prepares a very good version of one of our favorite Japanese lunches – katsu don ($11), or deep-fried pork strips on a bed of rice with egg. The pork, on occasion, can be a bit dry, but we blame that on low-fat American pork, not the preparation. Noodle, or udon dishes are also available – shrimp ($10.50) and vegetable ($7.50), as is the old standby, teriyaki ($11 for chicken, $14.95 for beef, $14.50 for salmon).

Prices are reasonable and the place is comfortable and cozy. At peak hours however, it can get a bit loud and service can slow down. Relax and put some Zen in your life. Have some sake or a 22-oz. Sapporo.

71. Rasoi

727 East Avenue (Hope Street)
Pawtucket, RI 02860
401-728-5500
www.rasoi-restaurant.com
Lunch, Dinner daily
Reservations
$$

Rasoi is in the fortunate strip mall (oh, excuse us, "Blackstone Place Plaza") right where Hope Street crosses into Pawtucket. Its next-door neighbor is LJ's Barbecue, one of our favorite places anywhere for 'cue – and on the other side is Garden Grill. From meat-eaters' paradise to veggie haven, Rasoi nests right in the middle and satisfies everyone. How lucky can a little neighborhood shopping center get?

If your impression of Indian restaurants was formed by low-budget curry parlors with beaded curtains and all-you-can-eat-for-$7.95 buffets, prepare for a pleasant attitude adjustment. The menu here is refined, traditional and creative and features dishes of diverse regions of India. Totally anonymous from the parking lot, Rasoi welcomes you with a cumin-scented waft of fragrance from the kitchen, which adds to your anticipation. Tables surround a small but lively central bar. Every table, every chair, and all the walls are united by a vibrant curry-and-tropical-blue color scheme which gives Rasoi a jazzy and appealing look. The design of the 85-seat restaurant and the bar provides patrons with an unobstructed view of the open kitchen. The place looks just great.

Rasoi chef Sanjiv Dhar, who started Kabob & Curry on Thayer Street in 1990, has created a menu with dishes from both north and south India. You'll find traditional, and familiar, northern dishes like chicken tikka lababdar ($12.99); the chunks of chicken are grilled then cooked in a fragrant, rich tomato-based sauce. Lamb saag ($13.99) is tender lamb stewed in a light spinach puree. There's also an extensive vegetarian menu based more on southern cuisine, with selections like okra masala ($9.99) and gujarati mango curry ($9.99). Biryani dishes – perfumed basmati rice with vegetables, chicken or mutton, cooked in a sealed pot – are exceptional. All the rice at Rasoi, by the way, is fragrant, tender and irresistible, perfect to soak up those rich tasty sauces.

Start your meal at Rasoi with the "Cauliflower 65." ($4.99) Well, maybe you should start by forgetting everything you thought you knew about cauliflower. These nugget-size wedges are marinated, then deep-fried so they're crunchy and golden on the outside. You dip them in a tamarind-tangy sauce that's hot and sweet and a little bit sour, too.

Prices at lunch are about half what they are at dinner, but even at dinner Rasoi is not expensive. The portions are generous, and the delicious rice has a tendency to swell during its passage through the upper regions of your gastrointestinal tract, providing a pleasing sensation of fullness. Throw in a crisp cold Kingfisher beer or two, and life is better than just good.

The service is friendly, courteous and organized. Even if you've always thought you "weren't crazy about Indian food," you should give Rasoi a try. It won't break the bank; the youthful and charming staff will help you choose foods that won't challenge your phobias, and what could be bad about a pleasant surprise?

72. Red Stripe
465 Angell Street (Wayland Square)
Providence RI 02906
401-437-6950
Breakfast, Lunch, Dinner daily
Brunch on weekends
Reservations
$$

Red Stripe created a need when no one knew it existed. Restaurateur Jaime D'Oliveira saw an opportunity for a bistro in Wayland Square and from the day it opened, the place has been packed. We love Red Stripe and crave the energy. It draws a handsome crowd who clearly like ogling one another.

But most of all, it feels comfortable. The warm red walls with beautiful tiles across the top, as well as the tiles across the black and white tile floor, the open kitchen, and the great bar provide a rich ambience. The menu offers classic French bistro dishes at American chain restaurant prices: onion soup, steak frites, frisée salad. Each evening Red Stripe features a special dinner listed across the bottom of the clear and detailed menu. Mussels prepared with any of several broth selections are a favorite and come in two sizes.

Some folks have the Midas touch, and some have the same luck with restaurants. Jaime D'Oliveira has a certain genius about this business and has created one attractive place after another. He is definitely Providence's version of a celebrity, and the cognoscenti know they MUST try everything he opens. His greater feat is keeping them coming back. We might hit Red Stripe a couple of times a week, and we know plenty of people who put our record to shame.

The food is reliable, flavorful and satisfying and the wine list is reasonably priced. What's not to like? Sometimes the noise gets painful to older ears, especially when youthful parties of 6 or more dine at a central table, but clearly the hip young crowd doesn't mind it a bit, and the regulars expect it and keep returning.

73. Ri Ra

50 Exchange Terrace (Downcity)
Providence, RI 02903
401-272-1953
www.rira.com
Lunch, Dinner daily
Reservations
$$

You really don't expect Ri Ra to feel so authentic, located as it is in a row of rather toney spots in the Union Station complex along Memorial Boulevard. But when you walk in, there you are in a real Irish pub. It's dark and a little bit seedy, and best of all, the seediness looks like the result of actual wear and tear, not some designer's expensive distressing of the woodwork and fixtures. Celtic music tweedles out of the speakers and a few of the folks at the booths and tables look as though they've been there a while.

The Guinness on tap ($4.75) is absolute perfection and the barman knows how to draw a proper pint. The food is typical

Irish pub fare, but it's good. Leek-and-potato soup comes with a couple of slices of soda bread and the soup is hearty, smooth, and tastes precisely of potatoes and leeks. An acid test for pub kitchens is fish-and-chips, found on the "Traditional Fare" portion of the menu. At Ri Ra, the fish is nicely crisped in its batter, and the fish itself is fresh and clean-tasting. It might be haddock, but we didn't ask. Underneath the two pieces of fish is a big pile of perfectly executed fries. The dish comes with lemon wedges, tartar sauce, which tastes homemade, or "Irish remoulade." Your server quite appropriately puts ketchup and malt vinegar in front of you with your order.

On Wednesday, burgers are half-price at lunch, and they're among the best in town. As long as you're working on a pint of stout, why not order the Guinness BBQ Burger, with "tangy Guinness BBQ sauce, melted cheddar, crispy onion rings"? Even at dinner, it's only $8.95 and you probably won't have to eat again for a day or two.

Ri Ra is fun, reasonable, and serves honest, well-prepared and tasty food. The only problem, really, is parking. If you're lucky, you might find a spot on Exchange Terrace – otherwise you'll probably end up in the lot behind the building (Ri Ra's entrance is on the end of 50 Exchange Terrace, perpendicular to the street), and it'll cost you. Recently we were there for lunch, which took us about an hour, and the parking bill was $6. If you can walk there from where you are, spend your parking money on a second pint. You'll still have change.

74. Rue de l'Espoir

99 Hope Street (Fox Point)
Providence RI 02906
401-751-8890
www.therue.com
Breakfast, Lunch, Dinner daily
Brunch on weekends
Reservations
$$ - $$$

Sometimes the Rue feels just right. On those days when we want a totally familiar setting and some comfort food, we are more than happy to head to the pink house on Hope Street. There is always crunchy, warm French bread passed around in baskets, and a good onion soup. This might be the only place in town that always serves quiche and crepes, and that might explain its immense popularity among seniors and the ladies who lunch. Try the perfect Salade Nicoise or the special soup of the day. Rue also has very pleasant service and has kept its standards through its quarter-century-plus run. That is, no doubt, the result of Deb Norman's firm hand at the helm and her daily oversight of operations.

Rue hops on the weekends with the younger set who literally line up out the door for the ever-popular Rue de L'Espoir brunch. Eggs Benedict, French toast, a panoply of omelettes and flapjacks, fresh fruits and mimosas, are all on the brunch menu which is served until early afternoon. Dinner features specials along with the excellent and creative chicken or duck and fish selections always accompanied by interesting sides beautifully presented.

We especially appreciate that the Rue has a quiet feel, we can hear the voices of our dining companions. Rue de l'Espoir has carved out a niche for itself over the years, and there is nary a long term resident who has not stopped in. For East Siders, especially, it's a trusted friend and neighbor who's always there for you.

75. Ruth's Chris Steak House

10 Memorial Boulevard (Downcity)
Providence RI 02903
401-272-2271
www.ruthschris.com
Dinner nightly
Reservations
$$$$

Somehow we know we are going to feel taken aback at Ruth's Chris by the sky high prices, but if we accept that, we have a terrific time. The location is fabulous, right there on the bowl of Waterplace Park in the G-Tech building; the décor is sophisticated, and makes us feel that Providence can compete with any big city. We know the food will be wonderful. It makes us a little nuts that a $48 piece of sirloin is described as "prime choice" - no such thing - but we figure it's part of the hype. Forty-eight bucks for a sirloin with butter sitting on a 500 degree plate, well, it makes you think. We move, on thinking our cocktail is swell, and are thrilled by the appetizers we sample: veal osso buco ravioli could be a meal in itself; the blue crab cakes with sizzling butter are flaky and delicious. Then we stumble again over a wine list that feels prohibitive. Even by the glass it is pricey. Oh dear. We sound so provincial. Let's get back to enjoying ourselves. The steaks arrive with great fanfare, and they do bring out the caveman in each of us. We devour each tasty bite. We are lucky people to be eating this dinner, luckier still when we are here to overlook a WaterFire. We skip the $8.00 baked potato and go for the shoestrings which are crisp and perfect. The creamed spinach is a tad gluey.

Desserts are tempting and we have to give them a try: "Chocolate Sin Cake" or crème brulée. We happily taste both. It has all in all been a hearty and sumptuous meal. But then…the bill. We suddenly have a taste of reality after our tasty food. Over $230 for two people! With plenty of steak house options in Providence, your decision to dine here becomes a matter of personal taste. No doubt, Ruth's Chris is a premiere American restaurant and one of the nicest we have here in town. So do go and enjoy, but go with your eyes and your wallet wide open.

76. Sawaddee Thai Restaurant
93 Hope Street (Fox Point)
Providence 02906
401-831-1122
www.sawaddeerestaurant.com
Lunch, Dinner daily, BYOB
$

A favorite with Brown and RISD students, Sawaddee Thai is a friendly, homey little spot on Hope Street a couple blocks north from Wickenden Street. Tiny tables, close together, mean that this is not a place for resolution of family feuds or intimate romantic dinners à deux. But for tasty, largely unthreatening Thai food at very reasonable prices, it's hard to beat.

When you walk in, you're IN. No vestibules, foyers or maitre-d stations get between you and your table. The only thing that might slow you down is the teaching assistant laboriously grading papers over a plate of pad thai, or the mom and her eight-year-old who are lingering over a shared food adventure. So you may have to wait a minute for a spot, especially at peak hours.

Soups are bracing and reviving, especially the tom-kha, which is a coconut-based broth prepared with your choice of chicken, vegetable or shrimp. Prices of many items depend on what you accessorize them with: this soup is $3, $3.20, or $3.75, for vegetable, chicken or shrimp.

Sawaddee offers no alcohol, but you're welcome to bring your own, a fine way to cut down on the cost of doing lunch or dinner. Dishes like the lab kai, chicken with lime juice, chili, coriander and scallions ($8.25), are available with from one to four-star heat ratings. At the four-star level, we'd definitely bring along a six-pack of our favorite beer for its cooling qualities.

Sawaddee has been pleasing Providence diners at the same location since 1996. As long as it maintains its standards, this little gem should be here for a long time.

77. Siena

238 Atwells Avenue (Federal Hill)
Providence RI 02903
401-521-3311
www.sienaprovidence.com
Dinner nightly
Reservations
$$$

Siena sizzles. When you walk in the door, you are immediately aware of laughter and voices and a room full of enjoyment. The food is tasty and priced right; the space is always full, the bar hops, and the patrons are so animated and engaged that you are happy before you get your first cocktail. The wine list offers many choices, fairly priced, and the wait staff is clearly prepared to answer queries about the selections.

Siena's menu lists its choices attractively in perfect Italian and provides great detail about preparation and accompaniments. The selection of antipasti is varied, and each offering is more tempting than the one before or after. The risotto is celestial (probably due to a shot of heavy cream), or you might choose the classic penne with vodka served with three jumbo shrimp. Try the delicious bistecca pepperonata, a red-wine, black pepper and balsamico marinated skirt steak grilled and finished with a tangy rich sauce for $18.95.

A bistro menu features grilled pizzas and cannellini beans in addition to calamari, a portabella mushroom dish and many pasta choices. All these offerings are seductive, creative and less expensive than the main menu. The space is attractive, the energy positive, the food exciting. The two brothers who opened Siena planned wisely, executed well and have acquired a loyal following.

78. Tazza

250 Westminster Street (Downcity)
Providence RI 02903
401-421-3300
www.tazzacaffe.com
Breakfast, Lunch, Dinner daily
$-$$

Sitting in Tazza in the heart of Downcity is reminiscent of being in SoHo. The space is utterly hip. The restaurant caffé sits on the corner of Westminster and Union Streets, surrounded by the gorgeous buildings of downtown Providence. Tazza is open for breakfast, lunch and dinner and provides great huevos rancheros and eggs benedict in the mornings, and paninis, pastas and salads from 11 a.m. until closing.

At lunch, we stopped in for an Italian panini and a chicken quesadilla, warm and oozing, with a fresh salsa and sour cream. The panini, which included salami, provolone, tomato and a side dish of hot peppers, was served with crunchy fat onion rings. Every staff member at Tazza is friendly and seems quite happy to be working there. And it does look like a great place to work, with the edgy architectural surroundings and the promise of live music in the evenings. Tazza is the ideal spot to stop in after browsing through Symposium books, or to meet friends for a late afternoon latte, but it also makes surprisingly tasty food. In the evenings Tazza turns into a cocktail lounge with entertainment that starts after the dinner hour, so it is also a terrific option before or after the theatre.

79. Temple Downtown

120 Francis Street (Downcity)
Providence RI 02903
401-919-5050
www.temple-downtown.com
Breakfast, Lunch, Dinner daily
$$-$$$

Back in 1929, workers on Providence's new Masonic Temple put down their tools and went home. The Masons had run out of money, so work was stopped until things got better. In 2004, work on the building began again, and in 2007 it opened its doors at last as a hotel, the Renaissance. Keeping its Masonic origins alive is the Temple Downtown, a spiffy and ambitious restaurant down a curving staircase from the hotel lobby.

Whether you enter from the street or the lobby, you'll pass through Temple's bar to reach the dining room, and you may want to pause to refresh yourself. The long and alluring bar features a list of cocktails equally long and alluring. The signature drink is the 33rd Degree, composed of brandy, Cointreau, fresh tangerine and lime juices. Other cocktails on the list are The Urban Farmer, which combines 8-year Bacardi with cucumber, ginger and lime, and the Dirty Little Secret, a mix of Pitu (whatever that is), Scotch-cut marmalade, fresh lemon juice and orange bitters.

Under the direction of chef Wayne Gibson, who has also cooked at XO, Lidia Shire's Biba, Inn at Castle Hill and Big Fish, the menu is eclectic and focuses on local bounty. Reviews are definitely mixed on the fusion broccoli rabe tempura but seafood is first-rate. Atlantic salmon with creamed corn and herb purée manages to keep flavors distinct while still coming together as a successful dish. (Mains are known as "templates" at Temple. Cute.) The Angus beef burger is frankly sensational, juicy, beefy, cooked accurately and served with organic cheddar, thick-cut bacon and an onion jam.

The menu at Temple can be confusing, although we're told that it's being reviewed. Under Chef Gibson, some of the original conceits that resulted in a plethora of gratuitous menu categories may be replaced by a more user-friendly format. But the innovative cooking, unique setting and reasonable prices that have already made Temple Downtown a real contender in the Providence dining derby.

80. 3 Steeple Street

125 Canal Street (College Hill)
Providence RI 02903
401-272-3620
www.3steeplestreet.com
Lunch Monday-Friday
Dinner Monday –Saturday
Reservations
$$-$$$

In 1792, Joseph Congdon built an ironworks at the corner of Canal and Thomas Streets. This site is the second oldest industrial site in America. Since then the building has undergone many uses, but our interest is in the current business which is a charming restaurant that pays homage to its lovely space. 3 Steeple Street has housed a restaurant for 28 years, owned the last eight by Julie and Billy Nahas

They have carefully lifted every scrap of plaster and debris off the shale walls, which adds immeasurably to wide plank floors, oversized glass windows and the overall ambience. It is particularly pleasing to sit in the ancient space and look out at the bustling city of Providence.

The restaurant is casual in feel, cozy and as welcoming to those who want a burger or salad as to those who are romantic enough to have the rack of lamb or the intriguing and fully seasoned Moroccan lamb stew. Other options include the plum-glazed duck breast or a dish of grilled marinated scallops wearing a jacket of crispy first rate bacon. There were at least five or six entrees we wanted to sample. Appetizers include a Caesar salad which you can order as a small plate or a large one for the table – a thoughtful, diner- friendly policy. The bar offers many brews offerings as well as wines by the glass or bottle. A plethora of dessert offerings tempted us, and so we tried two that were very good: pumpkin bread pudding and white chocolate ginger snap pudding.

Convenient to East Siders and downtown professionals, 3 Steeple Street deserves its many devoted regulars.

31. 10 Prime Steak and Sushi

55 Pine Street (Downcity)
Providence RI 02903
401-453-2333
www.tenprimesteak.com
Lunch Tuesday -Friday
Dinner nightly
$$$$
Reservations

Even before you walk through the swanky zebra striped door into 10 Prime Steak and Sushi, you immediately know that this is an upscale place: the restaurateurs have spent money on the décor; the service is top notch; the menu is edgy and inviting. But like an aging lady of the night, the décor has faded somewhat, and you want the place to be spruced up to keep it seductive. One way or another, 10 is still a happening place. The bar hops almost every night and on a recent icy winter Tuesday, there was nary a seat to be had at lunch time. It's an obvious favorite of business folk and attractive thirty-somethings.

On to the food: very, very good. The sushi menu offers top grade, tempting, perfectly prepared selections. We had sashimi, miso soup, crabcakes and the special prime steak salad of the day. The crabcake was ever so flavorful, albeit a tad over-breaded, but the steak was luscious, the sashimi stingingly fresh, the soup fragrant and satisfying. The tasty bread was a tempting crusty loaf with flecks of caramelized onion. The salt on the table was blue, or green, or red depending on where you sit. The 3-D glasses once required to read the menu are gone, but the innovative spirit survives. The restrooms are sound tracked with barnyard moos and bleats and in the men's room you hear what sounds like the St. Patrick's Day Parade with a bagpipe band marching right past the urinal.

These quirky innovations are standard for the Chow Fun Food Group, which puts the fun back into the restaurant experience. 10 Steak and Sushi may be the jewel in the crown for Chow Fun, which owns XO, Rick's Roadhouse, Citron, and Chinese Laundry. 10 specializes in fantastic and delicious cocktails, inventive menus, and great ingredients. We would always be delighted to eat at 10, but at the prices it commands, we want it to freshen its décor.

82. Tina's Jamaican Caribbean Restaurant

21 Atwells Avenue (Federal Hill)
Providence, RI 02903
401-490-4625
www.tinasjamaican.faithweb.com
Lunch, Dinner daily (Closed Sunday), BYOB
$

Tina is looking down at one of our plates. 'You didn't eat your greens!" she says. "It's not about the greens," the customer replies, abashed, "it's just me. I never eat my greens." Tina crosses her arms across her ample bosom. "This is Mama Tina talking. You need to get your vegetables!" Then she starts to laugh. "I never eat 'em either," she says.

Tina's Caribbean is that kind of place. If you had a friend whose mother was a really good cook -- and if she happened to be a Jamaican woman whose warmth filled up the room and she made jerk beef and chicken and shrimp and curried goat, then you have an idea of what's going on at Tina's.

This is real home cooking from the Islands. The flavors are rich and robust, and everything tastes fresh and just-made. When you walk into the rather plain but clean, bright dining room you see a refrigerated case in the back that holds water, sodas, and Tina's homemade soft drinks, including ginger beer and something called "Bedroom Bully." (We didn't ask.) The ginger beer tastes exactly like ginger – it's very lightly sweetened and hardly carbonated, so the first sip is a bit of a surprise. But it's refreshing and tastes great with Tina's cooking.

Caribbean-style shrimp is served with a "fiery" sauce and Tina uses homemade coconut milk in several dishes, including "MAMA TINA'S SPECIAL: Spicy Red Snapper steamed in coconut milk" ($15). All entrees come with the best Jamaican rice and beans, and remember to order fried plantain; you will forget you are on Atwells Avenue.

The jerk chicken ($10.00) is a rich dark mahogany, moist and spicy, but not too hot. Curries are mild for the most part. The curried goat ($10.50) in particular is delicious, the plate brimming with rice, fried plantain, greens of course, and the curry itself, fragrant and warming. The goat features cubes of on-the-bone meat, so tender that they're barely attached to that bone, tasting of what you might call lamb-and-then-some. When you're done, you want more. We thought of asking for seconds, but that would be unprofessional.

"Food So Great, You'll Scrape Your Plate!" is Tina's motto. You will, unless you have a problem with greens.

83. Tokyo
388 Wickenden Street (Fox Point)
Providence, RI 02906
(401) 331-5330
Lunch, Dinner daily, BYOB
Reservations
$- $$$

Aficionados looking for the best sushi in Providence should make a stop at this thoroughly Japanese spot on Wickenden Street. The sushi bar is to the left as you enter past the somewhat spartan dining room to the right. Take a seat at the counter and the waiter will hand you a list of a la carte sushi (nigiri) and sashimi selections that you check off yourself. You'll also get a regular menu for standard plates and combination dishes. Tokyo serves no alcohol, but the hot green tea goes well with the seafood.

Sashimi is fresh – some of the freshest and cleanest-tasting we've had in Providence – and attractively presented, usually with a mound of shredded daikon and a shiso leaf. Servings are generous and reasonably priced. The a la carte menu states prices for two pieces. Not all the selections are available on any given day, depending on what's in season.

Sushi, or nigiri, benefits from the same attention to quality as the sushi, but to our taste the portions are too large. Sushi is supposed to be eaten in one bite. Things can get ugly if you have to bite a piece in half, or saw it in two with your chopsticks. At Tokyo, the slices of seafood flop way over both ends of the rice ball. It is impossible to look at all composed if you have half a slice of fluke hanging from your lower lip, and if you stuff the whole thing in your mouth at once, it is just too much fish and rice to enjoy properly. The dish really should be savored as a delicacy. There is a trend towards "monster sushi" in the US, but one would think that the sushi chefs at Tokyo, where the atmosphere is so thoroughly Nipponese, would be above this fad.

Tokyo also offers a daunting selection of maki, or rolls, including a few that I'm certain are not at all traditional (Providence Roll? Rock 'n Roll?). One of these, along with a small salad or cup of miso soup, can make a very nice lunch. And the tab, if you go easy on the a la carte options, is very reasonable.

84. 242

242 Atwells Avenue (Federal Hill)
Providence, RI 02903
(401) 453-0242
www.twofortytwoprovidence.com
Dinner nightly
$$-$$$
Reservations

242 sneaked onto the Federal Hill scene in August of 2007 in the former Renaissance spot. The owner, David Mardirosian, who hails from Cape Cod, redecorated the space in a thoroughly attractive way and also improved the quality of the food and service. 242 is an upscale enterprise with good food, some innovative dishes, and moderate to high prices. The wine list also offers wines by the glass for about $9. The menu offers great options, with an equally inviting list of nightly specials.

Our salad from the menu was a Portaki salad, which combined portabella and shitaki mushroom slices with tomatoes, pancetta and mesclun in a light balsamic dressing. The chef prepares flatbread pizzas in at least a half dozen variations. We chose the Classico, with sausage, ricotta, marinara and basil and found it to be flavorful and crisp. Entrees for the evening included a pork chop with a tangy mustard sauce served over garlic braised spinach, a black pepper linguine with shrimp and creamy tomato sauce, and a strip steak which can be cut to order at $12 for 6 ounces and $2 for each additional ounce.

242 has what it takes to compete with its neighboring Siena and all the other places on Federal Hill. We could skip the sophomoric double entendre sexual references on the menu, with appetizers called "Foreplay," but we liked the food and the space. We believe that 242 will outlast many of the places that think a Federal Hill location means guaranteed success, but don't realize that quality is the determining factor.

85. Union Station Brewery

36 Exchange Terrace (Downcity)
Providence, RI
401-274-2739
www.unionstationbrewery.com
Lunch, Dinner Daily

Great chicken pot pie. There's a lot that's good about Union Station Brewery, but the chicken pot pie is stellar.

But let's start at the beginning. One of a complex of restaurants in the old Providence train station, Union Station Brewery is an actual brewery making very good beers and ales, including English-style cask-conditioned ales and seasonal brews that change every month or so. The restaurant is in a great space that is somehow exactly how a brewpub should look and feel. It's darkish but not dreary, oldish but not decrepit. And in the air is the unmistakable aroma of malt and hops.

You expect to find burgers and wings and nachos and Caesar salad on the menu, and you will. A surprise is the fine lobster bisque (cup, $3.99, bowl $4.99), that's smooth, creamy, light but rich and holds chunks of lobster meat and a nice hint of sherry. If you're there in wintertime and order the Holiday Red beer to go with your meal, you'll get a pint of smooth, malty, very lightly carbonated brew that is perfect with food. The complex toasty flavors are interesting on their own and complement just about everything on the menu.

Salads can really trip up a place like this when they're haphazardly assembled and glopped with gooey dressing.

Salads here are fresh and appealing. A recently sampled buffalo chicken salad ($9.29) came with crispy greens, battered fried chicken in a spicy sauce plus tomatoes, cucumbers, red onions and blue cheese crumbles. It was a big hit. But now a word about the chicken pot pie. There's not a dish on the traditional bar/brewpub menu that promises more and usually delivers less. Doughy, leaden crusts cover soupy, flavorless, over-floured stews of stringy chicken and way too many big chunks of carrot. Not here. A flaky crust shelters a dish of rich, chickeny sauce with big pieces of tender, moist chicken breast and just enough carrot and pea to lend a little color. This is one of those dishes that can satisfy a craving, and there's nothing better than knowing where a craving can be satisfied, and for only $9.99.

Good, consistent food, an appealing atmosphere, refreshing beers brewed on-premise, and friendly, responsive service make Union Station Brewery a highlight of the downtown dining scene. Every town needs at least one place like this, but are lucky if they have one. We're glad Providence got lucky.

86. Venda Ravioli

265 Atwells Avenue (Federal Hill)
Providence, RI 02903
(401) 421-9105
www.vendaravioli.com
Lunch daily
Reservations
$$

It's a grocery store. It's a salumeria. It's a butcher shop, a cheese store, a kitchen-tools emporium, a gift shop. And it's a restaurant. It's Venda Ravioli, and if there's not one in heaven, we're not going.

When you walk through the door on your first visit, you'll be visually overwhelmed. And much of what you see probably isn't what you came for. There's stuff hanging everywhere – boxes of panettone dangling from the ceiling like lampshades and Italian crockery displayed alongside the cheese graters and garlic presses and colanders. But the big island of food counters in the middle of the store is why people drive ALL THE WAY FROM ATTLEBORO to shop here. At the front, the charming, friendly staff make sensational sandwiches as they converse with you and with each other. Then there are prepared foods – eggplant parmigiana, meatballs, rabe, chicken cacciatore, chicken cordon bleu, chicken cutlets, chicken marsala. Not to mention the veal and the extraordinary pasta and vegetable combinations.

The cheese counter is one of the best in town, and the salumeria is ridiculous. We dare you to walk by without stopping. Prosciutto di Parma? Sliced so thin you can see through it. Vast selections of olive oils, balsamicos, San Marzano tomatoes, bread so fresh it's still warm, and prime meats at prices will make you think about renting an 18-wheeler and backing it up to the front door.

That's the most amazing thing about Venda Ravioli – at first glance, it looks suspiciously like a tourist trap. Too bright, too colorful, too many things. But it's the real deal. And everything is fairly priced.

We almost forgot -- you're here for lunch. If it's warm and sunny, you can dine outdoors. On those days, De Pasquale Plaza feels just like Italy. Or take a seat inside at a table right next to the butcher counter and admire the variety of impressive meats. Now look at the menu. Venda Ravioli makes, as you might suspect, its own pastas. The raviolis are especially good – if they're offering the ravioli stuffed with wild mushrooms, don't hesitate. Daily soup specials, like pasta e ceci ($3.95), are wonderful, as is just about anything made with beans. A bruschetta with escarole and cannellini beans, sampled on a recent visit, was a nice lunch all by itself; the escarole had just enough bite to complement the mellow beans and hearty bread. Entrees change frequently and are usually priced from $8.95 - $12.95. There's a short wine list – a generous glass of Chianti will be about $5.95.

Do some shopping before you leave. Your lunch won't be that expensive, and those marinated prime strip steaks in the meat case sure look good.

87. Waterman Grille
Four Richmond Square (Wayland Square)
Providence, RI 02906
401-521-9229
www.thegatehouse.com
Dinner nightly, Brunch on Sunday
Reservations
$$$

Waterman Grille has all the components of a great restaurant: a perfect location, plenty of free parking, and the backing and experience of the successful Newport Restaurant Group. The restaurant hangs over the Seekonk River where, as Rhode Islanders well know, The Gatehouse used to be. And those same native Rhode Islanders will tell you it's at the Red Bridge. The new owners opened this spot in April of 2007 with an inventive menu, a tasteful refurbishing of what was already gorgeous space, and enough buzz to keep folks lined up outside the door.

The food is quite good, and getting better all the time! The prices are quite reasonable, but it is more than possible to build quite a bill because of the many choices. The menu is divided into Daily Special Plates, Short Plates in the Tradition of Tapas, Share Plates, Grille Plates, Seafood Plates, Signature Plates, Salad Plates, Side Plates, and Wines By the Glass. So your bill will reflect your level of experimentation and whether you try tapas or dinner or both.

Among the appetizers, Humboldt Fog cheese with crisps and honeycomb ($4.50) was delicious. And tiny. We ordered two, which made it an expensive appetizer. Among the "Share Plates," Waterman Sliders ($7.95) were fun, and good: three little burgers with French-fried onion strings. Waterman Steak ($16.95), a hangar steak with a very zingy chipotle-bourbon aioli, was chewy but flavorful and cooked as requested. Order the braised pork shank if you can. A shared Caesar salad made everyone's list of favorites, and a dense, rich flourless chocolate cake topped the dessert selections we tried.

The wine list is interesting and offers a good selection of reasonably priced bottles.

The biggest problem for this restaurant is that everyone wants to sit on the outside porch overlooking the river and that is simply not a possibility. The policy is to honor the request when possible but to offer no guarantee. Given that, plan accordingly, knowing that you could have a lovely romantic dinner overlooking the twinkling lights, or you could be sitting in a busy, noisy barroom, eating at cocktail tables on bar stools, which though comfortable, may not be what you had in mind.

We will return again and again, because Waterman Grille is now one of the great places in Providence to dine.

88. Waterplace

1 Finance Way (Downcity)
Providence RI 02903
401-272-1040
www.waterplaceri.com
Lunch and Dinner Tuesday-Sunday
Brunch on Sunday
Reservations
$$-$$$

Waterplace has evolved into a fine restaurant. After many names and incarnations, from seafood, to Italian, to haute cuisine, and many different managers trying their own ideas, the Pinelli Marra group took over Waterplace in 2007 and stabilized the ship. Waterplace is in the middle of everything, and yet not. It is perched on the bank of Waterplace Park in its own odd little building, so it doesn't spring to mind when one thinks of downtown or the mall, and yet it is convenient to both. Valet parking after 5 p.m. makes it an easy spot to enjoy.

The food is classic American done with flavor and zing. A grilled romaine salad with crumbled chèvre, slow roasted tomatoes, olives and crunchy toasted soy nuts was both surprising and pleasing when dressed in a warm applewood bacon vinaigrette. We snapped up lobster fritters with a hint of tarragon and a Marsala chive remoulade like popcorn. Speaking of popcorn, there is even popcorn on the appetizer list, tossed in honey-chipotle butter. One entrée that was particularly successful on the winter menu was apple cider beer brined pork tenderloin with a mustard beer glaze. The sweet and tangy pork was complemented by a luscious cheddar spring onion corn pudding. Among desserts, the Fudgy Wudgy and Ooey Gooey were a chocolate layer cake and a carrot ice cream sandwich respectively. Both richly deserved their names.

On summer nights the patio at Waterplace is a lovely spot and on WaterFire nights, it sells out well in advance. But even on a midweek winter evening, it's a good place to try. The dining room is cavernous, but a successful effort to make it feel more cozy includes fabric hangings. The waterside dining area is especially inviting.

89. XO Steakhouse

125 North Main Street (College Hill)
Providence, RI 02903
401-273-9090
www.xosteakhouse.com
Dinner nightly
Reservations
$$$-$$$$

XO is a steakhouse, but with a difference. Unlike the big glossy chain steak places that have opened in Providence recently, XO feels local. When you walk in from North Main Street, you're right in the bar, a noisy, lively real-life BAR with people standing and drinking together because that's what they want to do. They're not waiting for a table; they're drinking and talking and doing the sociable things that good bars promote. There are tables in the bar, and you can even eat at the bar itself, but if you want to have a discussion over your meal, you'd be better off in the dining room.

The dining room is really two adjoining rooms, with a private wine room in the back. The tables are well spaced. The décor is, well, eclectic, but it all works and the tables are set with white linens and little flickering votives that turn out to be battery-powered. The menu begins by declaring, "Life is short. Order dessert first," and then offers not only steaks and chops, but an appetizing variety of choices, starting with cocktails. Instead of beginning with a glass of Pinot Grigio, why not treat yourself to an XO Mojito? You won't be sorry, and you can always have wine with your meal.

Some appetizers are huge. Consult with your server before you decide on, say, the Rhode Island calamari. There's enough squid on the plate to feed everyone in the room. Salads are also good appetizer choices, with Caesar ($8.50) and the XO Wedge Salad ($6.50) with goat cheese, not blue, are appealing options.

Steaks and chops are first-rate and all priced in the $30-$35 range – not bad for a serious steakhouse. The Colorado lamb rack is excellent: full of rich lamby flavor, nicely crisped on the outside and cooked exactly the way you ordered it. Steaks are aged Certified Black Angus, and of course you can get a great big porterhouse if a 14-oz. New York strip doesn't quite make it for you.

Our server steered us, gently, toward the truffle fries. They may be the best French fries in town, scented with truffle oil and dusted with Parmigiana, crunchy and irresistible, delivered in a tall silver paper-lined cone.

An impressive, wide-ranging wine list also offers by the glass choices at prices that average about $10.

Did you remember to order dessert first? Four words: Hot Molten Chocolate Cake. Order whatever you want, but make sure that someone at your table asks for it. Warm, intense, rich and runny, it's everything that chocolate is supposed to be but so rarely is.

You'll have a good time at XO. Chef Ben Lloyd is a perfectionist, and the food reflects his creativity and élan. The service is friendly and professional, although things can get a bit hectic on Saturday night. The well aged steaks and chops are outstanding, and the place has a nice lively buzz – without drowning out your every word.

90. Z-Bar

244 Wickenden Street (Fox Point)
Providence, RI 02906
401-831-1566
Lunch, Dinner daily
Reservations
$$-$$$

Z-Bar is on the corner of Hope Street and Wickenden Streets. Neighborhood people can walk there easily; motorists can usually find parking in one of their lots just east of Wickenden, and best of all, when they pass through the doorway, they can count on a very good experience.

Let's say it's a sunny Saturday afternoon and you're hungry. Your family has gone to the beach, and you've been working on your doctorate/doing stuff in the yard/waiting on hold at tech support/sleeping in. Mosey on down to Z-Bar. It's open and it's waiting for you. The long bar on the right is dim but not oppressively so and looks inviting, but since it's such a nice day, you decide to sit out back on the patio. The friendly server hands you a menu and points out the daily specials, listed on a blackboard nearby.

Often the menu includes mussel bisque. If it does, order it. It is one of the very best soups in Providence, a rich buttery dish of mussel essence, cream, a few little chunks of tomato and two or three mussels in their shells posed prettily in the center of the wide shallow bowl. Then dip some of Z-Bar's terrific warm crusty bread in the soup and sop it up – but save some for the olive oil dipping sauce with red pepper and grated Parmigiano.

Or have mussels in any form offered that day. Z-Bar, unlike many restaurants now boasting mussels on bistro-inspired menus, really knows its moules. They are invariably plump, juicy and full of that delicate flavor that mussels are supposed to have but so often don't. (Lately mussels have been missing. We're told it's a supplier problem. Let's hope it gets straightened out soon.)

There's a short but very appealing "Zangwich" list and if you're up for a burger, you won't be disappointed. The salads will please you too. You can't go wrong with the Caesar salad; it is especially good, with crispy romaine and a zingy dressing that benefits from a healthy smack of anchovy.

A wide selection of beers on tap beckons invitingly on a hot afternoon, but the Z-Bar wine list is good too, with wines by the glass that are interesting and change frequently. At Z-Bar your Guinness is poured professionally, with a creamy head still building as it's brought to you.

Look around. People are enjoying themselves. Your meal is delicious and attractively presented. The prices are reasonable. Maybe you should bring the family here for dinner.

91. Zooma Ristorante

245 Atwells Avenue (Federal Hill)
Providence, Rhode Island 02903
401-383-2002
www.zoomari.net
Lunch, Dinner daily
Reservations
$$$

Zooma would be on our list for its appearance alone. In summer, the deep purple façade is festooned with overflowing planters of purple flowers that frame the open seating. It is owner Joe DeQuattro's much appreciated gift to bustling Atwells Avenue.

All right, there you are loving the outside and so you just have to go in and give it a try. On a summer day, you can't beat sitting at one of the high tables in the open window, having some tuna carpaccio ($12) and watching the world go by. Zooma offers burgers and wood grilled pizzas, paninis and salads on the bistro menu and it also offers an extensive dinner menu. The triangular open kitchen dominates the large dining room in the back.

Pasta is a specialty at Zooma, like tagliatelle al funghi, a perfectly seasoned dish with white wine, garlic and fresh mushrooms, or try another tagliatelle, this one with braised rabbit. Polenta with grilled sausage and ragu is particularly good. The chef's emphasis on fresh ingredients is apparent throughout the dinner. A pan-seared chicken breast is fragrant with rosemary; roasted sea bass has a crunchy semolina crust. DeQuattro, who also owns Pane e Vino, is a connoisseur of wines, and his Zooma list arranges the different categories by lightest to heaviest, so if you don't know your Super Tuscan from your Valpolicella, you'll be able to negotiate your way through the list with ease. Most of the wines are from Italy you can choose from over 100 entries. Many bottles are priced in the $20-$30 range.

After eating at over 150 restaurants we made many mental lists. Where could we find the best burger, the best steak, where would someone want to pop the question, what are the various neighborhood restaurants like and what are some of the meals we will never forget? The results follow:

Most Romantic

These restaurants offer lovely or cozy surroundings, soft lighting, sensual food and privacy, where you and your beloved can spend a special evening, or, maybe, as in the case of Temple, a "naughty booth".

Cav
Gracie's
Guido's
La Laiterie
Local 121
Loie Fuller
New Rivers
Pane e Vino
Temple
Waterman Grill

Hip/Hot

We have plenty of traditional eateries in Providence, but we also have some that exude their own special energy. They are edgy or cool, or have somehow managed to be the magnet for different crowds – the RISD students, the twenty-somethings, the after work business crowd, the gay scene – and when you see them you'll get it immediately.

Cuban Revolution – both locations
DownCity
Julian's
Kurrents
Nicks on Broadway
Paragon
Red Stripe
Siena
Temple
10 Prime Steak and Sushi
XO

Low-Key

Many nights when you are sitting around in your jeans and you just want to go out for a casual meal. You don't want the white tablecloths and fancy food; you just want to get out of your kitchen and be comfortable at some local joint. These are the places we frequent the most and are grateful they are open on a regular basis.

Andreas
Blaze
Bravo
Broadway Bistro
Chilango's
Cuban Revolution
Guido's
Julian's
LJ's
Nick's
Oak
Paragon
3 Steeple Street
Z-Bar

Small plates, tapas & appetizers

If you just want small bites and not a big dinner, you will find some perfect spots . In most cases, the menu offers a wide array of small plates that won't eat a hole in your wallet. More and more diners order multiple appetizers instead of a first course and a main dish. Tapas menus offer variations on the Spanish bar-food staples. In Providence, the options are increasing. You can nibble your way through the openers at Temple or at a steakhouse like Ruth's Chris, or you can dig into the bivalves at the Providence Oyster Bar. At Cuban Revolution's two outposts you can choose from a gallery of tapas. Here are some of the top spots in town, for starters.

Bacaro
Citron
Cuban Revolution
La Laiterie
McCormick and Schmick
Red Stripe
Ruth's Chris
Temple

Big Deals

Several restaurants are designed to satisfy major expectations: family feasts, graduation dinners, visiting dignitaries, closings and openings. Both the tabs and the culinary ambitions are high. Locally trained chefs often manage their kitchens. Wine lists are extensive, cocktails are creative and plentiful, and many of these spots feature locally raised and sourced produce, meats and seafood. For a small city, Providence has a bounty of outstanding special occasion restaurants.

Al Forno
Bacaro
Café Nuovo
Capriccio
Costantino's
Gracie's
L'Epicureo
Mill's Tavern
New Rivers
10 Prime

Burgers

You can get one almost anywhere... but a really good burger is hard to find. From the creative (Temple) to the traditional (LJ's), here are some dependable sources.

Bravo Brasserie
Capital Grille
LJ's Barbecue
McCormick and Schmick
Napa Valley Grille
Paragon
Red Stripe
Ri Ra
Temple

'Za

How would we function without pizza? It fuels endless meetings, late-night crams, cheap dates and satisfies sudden cravings. Grilled, baked, thin-crust or deep-dish, Providence can deliver a pie for you. Our favorite suppliers are listed below – but there are many more. The important thing is to have a good one right around the corner.

Al Forno
Bacaro
Blaze
Bob & Timmy's
Camille's
Caserta's
Fellini's
Geppetto's
Kartabar
Olga's
242

High Steaks

Lately Providence has seen a wave of expensive steak houses wash into town. Are there too many for a city our size? Time will tell, but in the interim, steak lovers have a perhaps once-in-a-lifetime opportunity to surf this wave. All the places we list specialize in steak, but we should point out that almost every kitchen in town can serve you a steak if that's what you want. These places are cathedrals of beef, and their chefs are the archbishops.

Capitol Grille
Don Shula's
Fleming's
Mill's Tavern
Providence Prime
Ruth's Chris
10 Prime
XO

Fish: the Raw and the Cooked

For a port city, Providence suffers a shocking lack of good seafood places. Hemenway's holds up the high end, and then … where are the waterfront places where you can sit outside in the summer and watch the boats come in while you get lobster juices all over your shirt? See the list below for raw bars and sushi places we admire, but ask yourself why you have to drive out of town for a good shore dinner.

10 Prime
Haruki East
Hemenway's
McCormick and Schmick
Mill's Tavern
Providence Oyster Bar
Ran Zan
Tokyo

Meals at the Mall

Providence Place Mall is an island unto itself, offering a half dozen good options for meals. (We are not including the options in the food court offering Chinese, Indian, Japanese, French and American food, but here we list the places where you might want to sit down for dinner.) These all have appeal beyond the Mall and bring in plenty of diners from Downcity and the East Side as well as the 'burbs. Fire and Ice provides dramatic décor and food theatricality with its "you choose/we grill" option, Café Nordstrom is an oasis from shopping fatigue with food good enough to warrant a cookbook, the Cheesecake Factory is America's number one restaurant for a reason and Napa Valley Grille is competitive enough in fine dining to make it into our 91 Best list.

Joe's American Bar and Grill
Dave and Busters
Uno Chicago Grill
Fire and Ice
Smokey Bones Barbecue
Cheesecake Factory
Napa Valley Grille

Standout Dishes

We've tried many dishes, some of which knocked us out. We are still talking about these flavors and preparation, and textures.

Wild boar sausage at Nicks
Pork shank at Local 121
White bean bruschetta at Casa Christine
Pho at Pho Paradise
Natang at Angkor
Cow feet soup at Chapinlandia
Grilled pizza at Al Forno
Cauliflower 65 at Rasoi
Eggplant rollatini at Old Canteen
Chicken tinga tostada at Chilangos
Grilled romaine salad at Waterplace
Crispy beef at MuMu

Road Trips

When you feel like getting out of town, but not too far out of town, these are the few places we highly recommend. All are within a 25 minute drive from Providence. Therefore, we do not list Newport restaurants.

1149
Division Street
Warwick, RI
401-884-1149
Handsome appealing interior, world class chef, great menu which offers terrific food at a range of prices.

HON
780 Reservoir Avenue
Cranston, RI
401-946-218887555
Some of the best Vietnamese food you will ever taste in this small undistinguished Cranston location. Wine and beer available. Try the Pho and the Banh Hoi, or the Vietnamese Crepe, or the Pork in garlic sauce, or…..

N-Joi
39 Phoenix Avenue
Cranston, RI
401-944-7770
Sophisticated, metropolitan décor and sensational food at

this mid-sized restaurant in a Cranston strip mall. Urban feel, suburban prices.

Persimmon
31 State Street
Bristol, RI
401-254 7474
Chef Champe Speidel has made a BIG name for himself in this little restaurant, with his own personal style and sophisticated, exciting food.

Le Central
483 Hope Street
Bristol, RI
401-396 9965
This is one of those places we would eat at every night if it were in our neighborhood. Chef Jesse James uses his impressive experience and undisputed talent to our advantage. Great bistro food, first rate ingredients, very reasonably priced.

DeWolf Tavern
Thames Street Landing
Bristol, RI
401-254-2005
Dramatic surroundings in this old rum warehouse on the water, a world class chef, a sophisticated American menu with Eastern influence.

Twin Oaks
100 Sabra Street
Cranston, RI
401-781-9653
We can't leave out this RI favorite where enormous portions of steaks and seafood are served in traditional ways at moderate prices. After 75 years, there is still a waiting line for tables at this famous spot, despite its 650-seat capacity.

OUR PERSONAL TOP TEN LISTS

Deborah
Bravo
Cav
Chilangos
Fleming's
Gracie's
Mill's Tavern
New Rivers
Nicks on Broadway
Providence Prime
Venda Ravioli

John
Al Forno
Cav
Chez Pascal
Gracie's
La Laiterie
Local 121
Mill's Tavern
Nicks on Broadway
Pho Paradise
Venda Ravioli
Z-Bar

PET PEEVES

We know what you're thinking: how could anyone whose life consists of eating out possibly have a peeve? Well, we have a few, and they may be yours, too.

Let's start with **no-reservations policies**. Of course, a little storefront place on the Cranston line doesn't need to take reservations. People come in, sit down, eat, leave. Tables turn over quickly. No one gets upset. But what about restaurants that get upwards of $50 a customer for dinner and still make their patrons stand around hoping they'll get in? That's unnecessary and unconscionable. Some of our very favorite places in town do that, and we don't get it. Restaurateurs will tell you that they get stuck holding tables for people who don't show up. Take a credit card with a deposit. How hard is that? The best restaurants on earth have solved this one by putting their customers first. The best restaurants in Providence should do the same.

On a recent evening, we came into a relatively empty restaurant, La Laiterie to be exact, to be told we had to sit at the bar. We asked for one of the four tops (there were 3) to be split into 2 tops, as they are throughout the restaurant. A rather self-important maitre d' asserted this was impossible as they reserved them for larger groups. After we ate our dinner, conversing in the company of our bartender and fellow companions, we left noting that all 3 four tops were still empty.

Here's another: **mammoth portions.** This is really a Rhode Island thing, probably a legacy of the whole abbondanza culture of Federal Hill. (We also can't stand the itsy-bitsy portions of some very precious restaurants of the haute cuisine variety, but happily Providence doesn't boast any of those. Yet.) Too many restaurateurs here confuse quantity for quality, or at least value, and fail to recognize that a mountain of food is an appetite suppressant. Presentation is critical, but the idea is to make the food look appealing, not intimidating. Some steak houses offer their sirloins and ribeyes in different weights. Maybe platters of eggplant parmigiana should be offered the same way.

Paying for parking irks us, too. In a city where you can park free right on the street at many places, adding six bucks or so to your dinner tab because the only option is a private lot seems harsh – especially when that's the rate you get after your claim check has been stamped by the restaurant! On Atwells, many places offer free valet parking, a sane response to a non-parking-friendly environment. It should be more widespread.

In upscale restaurants with ambitious menus and prices to match, there's no excuse for **unprofessional service**. Any restaurateur who hasn't read Danny Meyer's book, *Setting the Table: The Transforming Power of Hospitality in Business*, should take a look. Meyer's New York restaurants, including Union Square Café and Gramercy Tavern, are among the most popular and admired in town. But it's not all about the food. For his customers, the experience is about feeling welcome followed by discreet attention. That means servers don't introduce themselves by name. They know every dish on the menu. Tables are bussed promptly so that courses have a place to go when they arrive. Servers are available but not intrusive. The dining room staff works to create an atmosphere of calm and welcoming competence so that you can properly appreciate your meal. Salt and pepper are on the table. The ketchup arrives with the hamburger; the cream and sugar come with the coffee. All diners are served simultaneously, and no dish is cleared until the last diner is finished eating. You can't enjoy your food, no matter how well prepared, if you're all stressed because you can't find your waiter. This is so basic, but it's amazing how many places with high-flying kitchens don't understand that the front of the house is as important as the back. Maybe more so.

Ads with naked women with black strips over their nipples, or menus with headings like Foreplay or Under the Sheets are totally offensive. Not only do they seem gratuitous and sophomoric, but they have nothing to do with the enterprise of serving good food. Moreover, they imply we are heading for a strip joint rather than what turns out to be an attractive, decent restaurant.

Providence restaurants need to **get a bit more imaginative with their menus.** If we did a spread sheet on dishes offered, we would find many, many duplicates. We know everyone wants the option for a Caesar salad with chicken, but we would welcome many other salad options on the menus. The same goes for meatloaf and veal parmigiana. It is fine to offer them, but give the chef a little chance to shine with some new dishes. We have heard this complaint from many folks who eat out all the time, and turn to the ethnic restaurants for a little variety. If Providence wants to remain prominent in the culinary world (which it is), we need new options on a regular basis.

College Hill

Andreas - **3**
Blaze - **7**
Chinese Laundry -**23**
Hemenway's - **36**
Kabob and Curry -**39**
Kartabar - **40**
Mill's Tavern - **51**
New Rivers -**54**
Paragon - **62**
Parkside - **63**
3 Steeple Street - **81**
XO - **89**
Phonatic - **64**

Downcity

Agora - **1**
Bravo - **10**
Café Nuovo -**12**
Capitol Grille -**15**
Capriccio -**16**
Cav -**19**
Citron - **24**
Don Shula's - **27**
DownCity - **28**
Fleming's - **30**
Gracie's - **33**
L'Epicureo - **45**
Local 121 - **47**
McCormick & Schmick - **49**
Napa Valley Grill -**53**
Olga's -**58**
Pot au Feu - **67**
RiRa - **73**
Ruth's Chris Steakhouse -**75**
Tazza - **78**
Temple - **79**
10 Prime Steak and Sushi - **80**
Union Station Brewery - **85**
Waterplace -**88**
Cuban Revolution - **26**

Federal Hill

Angelo's - **4**
Blue Grotto - **8**
Bob and Timmy's - **9**
Caffe Dolce Vita - **13**
Camille's -**14**
Casa Christine - **17**
Cassarino's - **18**
Costantino's - **25**
Geppetto's - **32**
Mediterraneo - **50**
MuMu - **52**
Old Canteen - **57**
Opa - **59**
Pane e Vino - **61**
Providence Oyster Bar - **68**
Providence Prime - **69**
Siena - **77**
Tina's Carribbean- **82**
242 Atwells - **84**
Venda Ravioli - **86**
Zooma - **91**

Fox Point

Al Forno - **2**
Angkor - **5**
Bacaro - **6**
Guido's - **34**
Kurrents - **41**
Pakarang - **60**
Rue de l'Espoir - **74**
Sawadee - **76**
Tokyo - **83**
Z Bar - **90**

Hope Street

Blaze - **7**
Chez Pascal - **21**
Garden Grill - **31**
India - **37**
LJ's Barbecue - **46**
Oak - **56**
Pizzico - **66**
RanZan - **70**
Rasoi - **71**

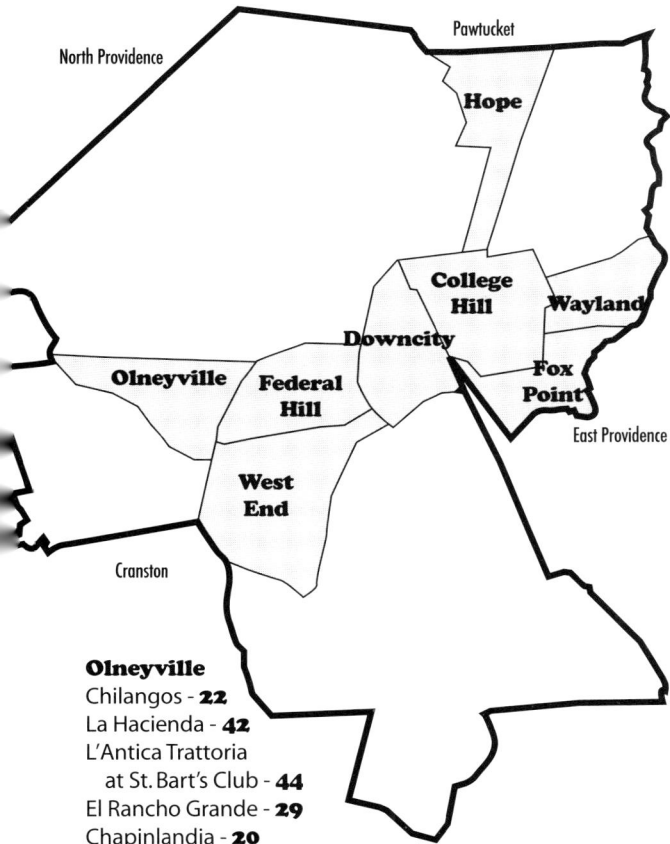

Pawtucket

North Providence

Hope

College Hill

Wayland

Downcity

Olneyville

Federal Hill

Fox Point

East Providence

West End

Cranston

Olneyville
Chilangos - **22**
La Hacienda - **42**
L'Antica Trattoria
   at St. Bart's Club - **44**
El Rancho Grande - **29**
Chapinlandia - **20**

Wayland Square
Haruki - **35**
La Laiterie - **43**
Red Stripe - **72**
Waterman Grille - **87**

West End
Broadway Bistro - **11**
Julian's - **38**
Loie Fuller - **48**
Nick's on Broadway - **55**
Pho Paradise - **65**

COLLEGE HILL

FOX POINT

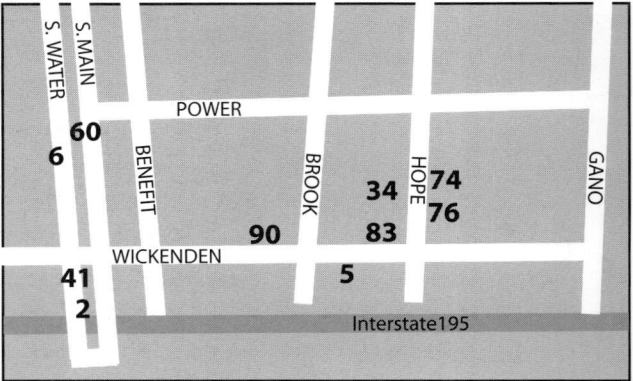

HOPE STREET

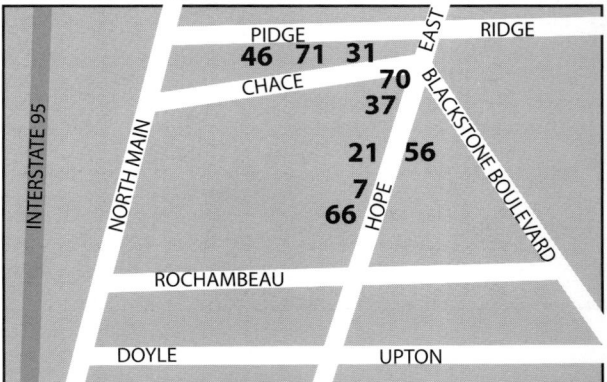

114

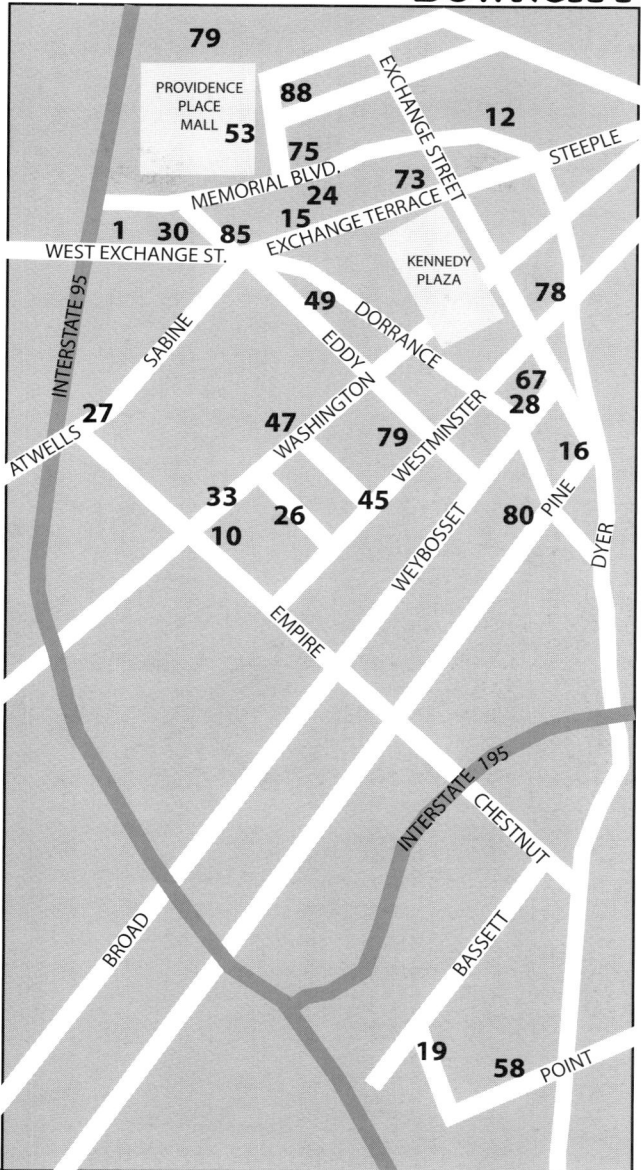

79

PROVIDENCE
PLACE
MALL
53

88

EXCHANGE STREET

12

STEEPLE

75

MEMORIAL BLVD.

24

73

1 30 85

15

EXCHANGE TERRACE

WEST EXCHANGE ST.

KENNEDY
PLAZA

INTERSTATE 95

49

DORRANCE

78

SABINE

EDDY

67
28

ATWELLS

27

47

WASHINGTON

79

WESTMINSTER

16

PINE

33

26

45

WEYBOSSET

80

DYER

10

EMPIRE

INTERSTATE 195

CHESTNUT

BROAD

BASSETT

19

58

POINT

FEDERAL HILL

OLNEYVILLE

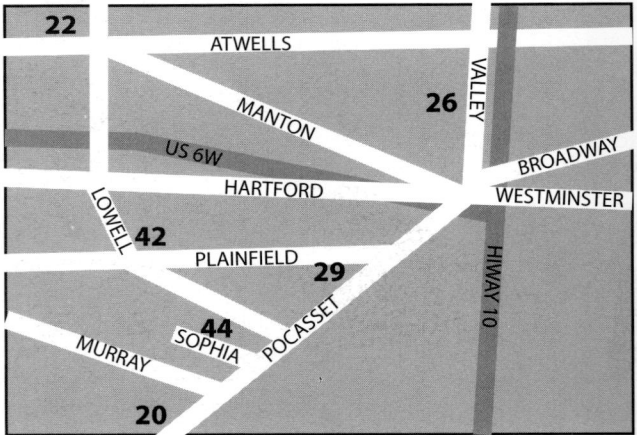

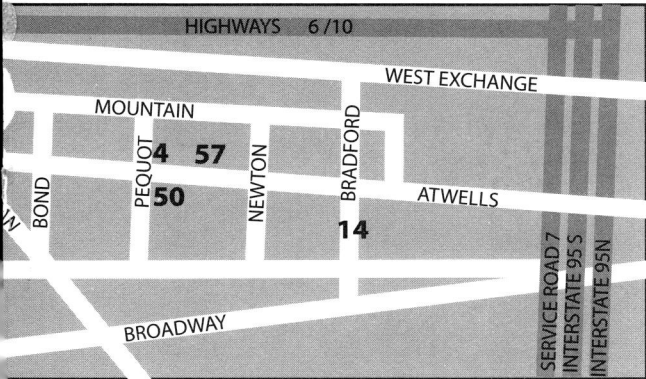

HIGHWAYS 6/10

WEST EXCHANGE

MOUNTAIN

PEQUOT

4 57

50

BOND

NEWTON

BRADFORD

ATWELLS

14

BROADWAY

SERVICE ROAD 7

INTERSTATE 95 S

INTERSTATE 95N

WAYLAND SQUARE

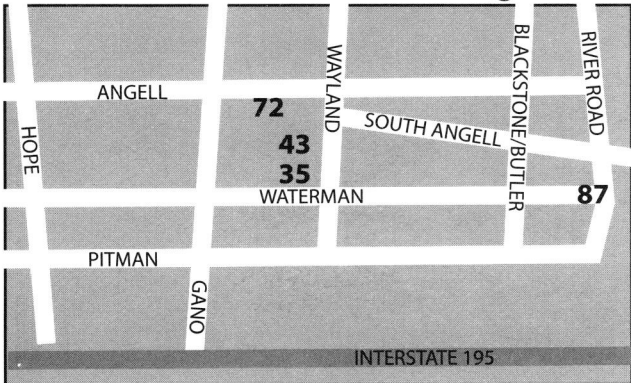

ANGELL

HOPE

72

43

35

WATERMAN

WAYLAND

SOUTH ANGELL

BLACKSTONE/BUTLER

RIVER ROAD

87

PITMAN

GANO

INTERSTATE 195

WEST END

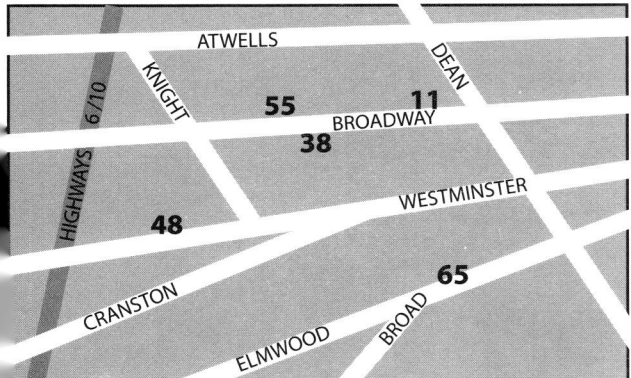

ATWELLS

KNIGHT

DEAN

55

11

38

BROADWAY

HIGHWAYS 6/10

48

WESTMINSTER

CRANSTON

65

ELMWOOD

BROAD

...but in the end,
who knows better than you do!!!

(add your own restaurant notes here)

_____

_____

_____

_____

_____

_____

_____

_____

_____

_____

_____

_____

_____

_____

_____

_____

_____

_____

_____

_____

_____

_____

_____

_____

_____

_____

_____